The Terry Lectures

LIFE AFTER FAITH

Other Volumes in the Terry Lectures Series Available from Yale University Press

The Courage to Be Paul Tillich

Psychoanalysis and Religion Erich Fromm

Becoming Gordon W. Allport

A Common Faith John Dewey

Education at the Crossroads Jacques Maritain

Psychology and Religion Carl G. Jung

Freud and Philosophy Paul Ricoeur

Freud and the Problem of God Hans Küng

Master Control Genes in Development and Evolution Walter J. Gehring

Belief in God in an Age of Science John Polkinghorne

Israelis and the Jewish Tradition David Hartman

The Empirical Stance Bas C. van Fraassen

One World: The Ethics of Globalization Peter Singer

Exorcism and Enlightenment H. C. Erik Midelfort

Reason, Faith, and Revolution: Reflections on the God Debate Terry Eagleton

Thinking in Circles: An Essay on Ring Composition Mary Douglas

The Religion and Science Debate: Why Does It Continue? Edited by Harold W. Attridge

Natural Reflections: Human Cognition at the Nexus of Science and Religion Barbara Herrnstein Smith

Absence of Mind: The Dispelling of Inwardness from the Modern Myth of the Self Marilynne Robinson

Islam, Science, and the Challenge of History Ahmad Dallal

The New Universe and the Human Future: How a Shared Cosmology Could Transform the World Nancy Ellen Abrams and Joel R. Primack

The Scientific Buddha: His Short and Happy Life Donald S. Lopez, Jr.

LIFE AFTER FAITH

THE CASE FOR

SECULAR HUMANISM

PHILIP KITCHER

Yale

UNIVERSITY PRESS

New Haven and London

Published with assistance from the Mary Cady Tew Memorial Fund.

Yale University Press books may be purchased in quantity for
educational, business, or promotional use. For information, please e-mail
sales.press@yale.edu (U.S. office) or sales@yaleup.co.uk (U.K. office).

Set in Adobe Garamond and Gotham type by IDS Infotech Ltd.,
Chandigarh, India.
Printed in the United States of America.

Library of Congress Cataloging-in-Publication Data
Kitcher, Philip, 1947–
Life after faith : the case for secular humanism / Philip Kitcher
pages   cm — The Terry lectures
Includes bibliographical references and index.
ISBN 978-0-300-20343-1 (alk. paper)
1. Secular humanism. I. Title.
BL2747.6.K58 2014
211'.6—dc23   2014010384

A catalogue record for this book is available from the British Library.

This paper meets the requirements of ANSI/NISO Z39.48-1992
(Permanence of Paper).

10 9 8 7 6 5 4 3 2 1

For Sully
and his parents,
with love

The Dwight Harrington Terry Foundation Lectures on
Religion in the Light of Science and Philosophy

The deed of gift declares that "the object of this foundation is not the promotion of scientific investigation and discovery, but rather the assimilation and interpretation of that which has been or shall be hereafter discovered, and its application to human welfare, especially by the building of the truths of science and philosophy into the structure of a broadened and purified religion. The founder believes that such a religion will greatly stimulate intelligent effort for the improvement of human conditions and the advancement of the race in strength and excellence of character. To this end it is desired that a series of lectures be given by men eminent in their respective departments, on ethics, the history of civilization and religion, biblical research, all sciences and branches of knowledge which have an important bearing on the subject, all the great laws of nature, especially of evolution . . . also such interpretations of literature and sociology as are in accord with the spirit of this foundation, to the end that the Christian spirit may be nurtured in the fullest light of the world's knowledge and that mankind may be helped to attain its highest possible welfare and happiness upon this earth." The present work constitutes the latest volume published on this foundation.

The organism, its decay, the indestructibility of matter, the law of the conservation of energy, development, were the words that had replaced his former faith. These words and the concepts connected with them were very well suited to intellectual purposes, but they gave nothing for life, and Levin suddenly felt himself in the position of a person who has traded his warm fur coat for muslin clothing and, caught in the cold for the first time, is convinced beyond question, not by reasoning but with his whole being, that he is as good as naked and must inevitably die a painful death.

—*Leo Tolstoy, Anna Karenina*

Contents

Preface   xi

1 Doubt Delineated   1
2 Values Vindicated   27
3 Religion Refined   61
4 Mortality and Meaning   95
5 Depth and Depravity   123

Sources   161
Index   169

Preface

When I was five years old, I began singing in the church choir. The boy trebles had a standard pay scale: we received small amounts for rehearsals, slightly larger fees for services, and bonuses for special occasions—a florin (two shillings) for a funeral, half a crown (two shillings and sixpence) for a wedding, showing apparently that joy pays better than grief. Most of my income was to be saved, deposited for me in a Post Office Savings Account, but I was allowed to keep a little as pocket money.

For the next twenty-one years I continued to sing church music (soon no longer paid), attending services regularly—in my boarding school days even at the rate of eight a week. I have seen a lot of light fall through stained glass windows, have felt the sonorities of the Authorized Version (the King James Bible) press themselves into my linguistic consciousness, have dozed through a good number of sermons and been inspired by others. Above all, I have been caught up in the music, from the minor compositions of the Anglican rite (Wood and Darke and Stanford) to the magisterial works of the Western tradition (from Josquin to Britten and beyond). As a teenager, I was unusually lucky, for, instead of abruptly breaking, my voice sank gently over several years, allowing me to sing the four main parts (soprano, alto, tenor, and bass) in the course of its descent. So I have represented all four voices in Handel's *Messiah* and in Brahms's *Deutsches Requiem*.

In my early teens, my faith began to slip, underwent a few bouts of renewal, and then disappeared for good. Since I was at school, at "the religious, royal, and ancient foundation of Christ's Hospital," there was no option of skipping services, and I continued to sing, even fortissimo in the appropriate places, while mumbling or avoiding the spoken responses. The pattern was set, and neither as an undergraduate at Cambridge nor as a graduate student at Princeton did it seem to me necessary to abandon the music I loved simply because I no longer believed the words. Only later, when I discovered other, less time-consuming opportunities for amateur music-making, did my Sunday morning habits fall into line with my intellectual convictions.

Throughout my career as a teacher of philosophy, I have often returned to thinking about religion, trying from various angles to elaborate my conviction about some things and my lack of conviction about others. An early book scrutinizing the Creationist campaign against Darwin (*Abusing Science*) seemed incomplete without a final chapter on the relations between evolution and religion—and Patricia Kitcher and I duly co-wrote one. Over the years, our discussion came to seem unsatisfactory to me (and my co-author was far quicker than I in discerning its shortcomings). I have since tried again—and again—to explain why I take religious doctrines to have become incredible, and why, despite this fact, I resist the now dominant atheist idea that religion is noxious rubbish to be buried as deeply, as thoroughly, and as quickly as possible.

When the Terry Lectures Committee honored me with the invitation to deliver a set of lectures, I immediately saw this as a welcome opportunity to speak—and write—about secular humanism as a positive position. In the lectures as originally delivered, and in my subsequent reworking of them, I have attempted to combine philosophical reflection and analysis with my abiding sense that there are valuable aspects of the religion I long ago abandoned. My attitude is not, I hope, mere sentimentality or nostalgia, nor is it purely an aesthetic appreciation of the words, the music, the architecture, and the paintings. Deeper even than the joys sparked by the artistic triumphs of religion lies a vivid memory of the ways in which belonging to a religious community transformed the lives of people I knew well in my childhood. The church in which I originally sang has no great aesthetic merit—it is an ugly brick building—but for the congregation that attended it, Sunday after Sunday, people for whom life was often hard and who counted the pennies and the shillings, it was a place of comfort, solace, and inspiration. Today, in the poorer areas of northern Manhattan, not far from where I now live, churches and mosques and synagogues continue to play a similar role.

The manifestos of contemporary atheism frequently delineate the evils that have been done in the name of religion. Critics of religion document the ways in which hatred and violence have been born of religious intolerance. They show how rigid dogma has confined, and continues to confine, many lives, and sometimes they even try to help relax the constraints: for example, Daniel Dennett, working with Linda LaScola, has done valuable and humane work in assisting clergy who have lost their faith. Yet the atheist movement today often seems blind to the apparently irreplaceable roles religion and religious community play in millions, if not billions, of lives. The central purpose of this book is to show how a thoroughly secular perspective can fulfill many of the important functions religion, at its best, has discharged. I hope to explain how a secular world is not something to be frightened of, how it might provide even for those who rightly take themselves to be most vulnerable to the vicissitudes of life.

In thinking my way through these issues, I have incurred many debts. Since I came to Columbia in 1999, Wayne Proudfoot has been a wonderful interlocutor, and numerous conversations and sets of written comments have left their mark on my thinking. Kent Greenawalt and Taylor Carman have provided me with large amounts of excellent advice. Conversations with Edward Mendelson have constantly challenged me to consider issues more deeply. The late Sidney Morgenbesser guided me to James and Dewey, and talking with him transformed my approach to philosophy. Students in my courses on science and religion have posed many important questions and raised constructive criticisms. Beyond Columbia, exchanges with Jerry Coyne and Dan Dennett (both firmer than I in their rejection of religion) have always been illuminating.

I am grateful to the Yale community for its warm hospitality, and to the audiences at the Terry Lectures for their interest and for their responses. Tamar Gendler, Paul Bloom, and especially Shelly Kagan prompted me to do some serious rethinking. The manuscript of the lectures was read by three referees for Yale University Press, all of whom offered perceptive comments that have led to significant revisions. Since one of those referees identified himself as Thomas Nagel, I can also thank Tom for the many things I have learned from him over four decades.

Several friends read the penultimate draft, giving me advice, encouragement, and sometimes detailed commentary. I am deeply grateful to Lynne Rudder Baker, Michael Gordin, Rainer Hegselmann, Bruce Robbins, and Charles Taliafero. Above all, I would like to thank George Levine, for his remarkably sensitive reading, his wise counsel, and his dedication to making space for secular humanism as a positive project.

Jean Thomson Black has been a most supportive editor, and has helped me to see where my formulations needed clarification and further development. As always, Patricia Kitcher has been the best of critics, and I owe her more than I can say.

LIFE AFTER FAITH

ONE

DOUBT DELINEATED

|

Secular humanism begins in doubt, but doubt should be only the beginning. For anyone who has lived under the sway of religion, the rejection of religious commitment leaves a vacuum demanding to be filled. Tolstoy's Levin speaks for millions who have lost a once-cherished faith and who are now tormented by their nakedness and vulnerability. However forceful or well-informed or eloquent the voices of atheism may be, however convincing their denunciations of the devastating effects of religious intolerance, mere denial leaves human needs unaddressed: the fully secular life cries out for orientation. Nor is it enough to extend the atheistic critique with a hymn to the glory of scientific understanding. Listening to the choir of contemporary atheists, it is easy to sympathize with William James's pithy characterization of the fervent unbeliever: "He believes in No God and worships him."

If secular humanism is to be *lived*, and to be understood as a fully rewarding way for human beings to live, the humanist perspective requires positive elaboration. Purely negative broadsides arouse reactive doubts, to the effect that secularists have ignored pervasive aspects of people's lives, so that the human has entirely disappeared from view. Clusters of comfortable intellectuals may be satisfied by secular humanism, but people not primarily focused on the search for knowledge, or people bruised by the vicissitudes of the world, will need substitutes for the guidance that trenchant objections have undermined.

My principal aim in this book is to explore one way of articulating secular humanism, so as to answer complaints that it allows only an impoverished form of human existence. I shall try to understand the sources of the sense of loss, and to respond to them. The underlying concerns are sometimes intellectual, sometimes practical and social. A secular *worldview* is often taken to be inadequate for grounding claims that some things are valuable or are morally required of us, and that others are worthless or to be prohibited. It is allegedly unable to provide comfort in the face of death, to account for the meaningfulness of human life, and to capture the richness and depth of human experience. A secular *world* is supposedly bereft of institutions and forms of daily life that support important forms of conduct and community. Without the social structures provided by religion, valuable types of human relationship disappear and there is often no space for the joint pursuit of shared goals and values. I shall try to show how the intellectual questions can be answered, and how we can take steps to address the practical problems. Yet it is only right to acknowledge, from the beginning, that a fully rewarding secular world cannot be built in a day. The world's major religions, at their best, have lavished centuries on responding to the human needs of the faithful (and even, occasionally, to those of unbelievers as well). Attempts to devise secular substitutes can learn from their experiments and from their successes. So, I suggest, secular humanism does well to attend sympathetically to the most enlightened versions of religion. Listening is, of course, harder when the voices of atheism insist on treating religion as an undifferentiated mass of rubbish, to be carted away as thoroughly and as speedily as possible.

Although my primary purpose is the construction of a positive perspective, it will be useful to start by reviewing what I take to be the most powerful reasons for secularist skepticism. Secular humanism *begins*, after all, with doubt.

II

What kinds of doubt? About religion, of course—but to say that only provokes a further question: What exactly is religion, or what counts as "a religion"?

A popular, but incautious, answer proposes that religions consist of bodies of doctrine about the existence and characteristics of special kinds of beings—deities—who deserve our worship and service because of their impressive attributes. The deepest difficulty with this answer is that doctrines, articles to be believed by the devout, need not be central to all forms of religion. A more straightforward problem is that not all of the many religious practices of human cultures are centered on deities: some focus on spirits, or ancestors, or even on impersonal "forces," with which it is important for people to align themselves. Setting the deeper concern aside for the moment, an obvious refinement of the incautious proposal will address the straightforward objection: Religions are distinguished by their invocation of something beyond the mundane physical world, some "transcendent" realm, and they offer claims about this "transcendent." Although the term thus introduced is as vague as it is popular, the intent in using it is clear: the transcendent is radically different in kind from mundane reality, and (perhaps) not accessible via the methods people use to investigate other aspects of nature.

All around the world, religious people avow doctrinal statements, and thereby offer their preferred versions of what the transcendent is like. They declare that God made a covenant with Abraham, or that an angel who visited the Prophet commanded him to recite the divine message, or that Jesus rose from the dead (to take three salient examples). Part, but only part, of secular humanist doubt consists in the denial that any of these statements (or any of their counterparts in other religions) are true.

That denial cannot be understood, nor its grounds appreciated, without first considering what the statements are supposed to mean. A familiar distinction separates "literal" construals of religious claims, usually presented in particular scriptures, from alternative interpretations that are metaphorical, or allegorical, or poetic. The division, however, is only a crude way of marking the ends of a continuum. At one pole are readings supposing that an ancient Mesopotamian pastoralist was once visited by an imposing old man with a long white beard (in the manner of Blake), that a Meccan estate manager had repeated encounters in the desert with a large gleaming figure outfitted with magnificent wings, and that the son of a carpenter from Nazareth was completely dead and later alive again, where the criteria for life and death are those of current medical practice. Perhaps there are Jews and Muslims and Christians who subscribe to precisely these interpretations—just as there are some who believe that the world was created in six periods of exactly twenty-four hours, and that all major kinds of plants and animals were formed at the very beginning. Most people who profess these faiths probably do not intend anything so detailed and specific when they make their credal declarations. They allow that ordinary descriptions are incomplete, that the doctrines contain "mysteries."

Many religions, including the three Abrahamic versions of monotheism, supply a rich body of statements for the faithful to interpret and to affirm. Idealizing from the messy facts of human psychology, we might assign each religious believer a *doctrinal profile*, resulting from the level of detail and specificity with which she reads each of the doctrinal statements. Sometimes she may import all of the everyday implications of the words used: "Jesus wept" is construed as claiming that a particular historical figure shed tears on a particular occasion. In other instances, she may retreat from the commonplace allusions and implications: Muhammad, in the Meccan desert, had an extraordinary experience in which what he conceived as an outside source inspired him to repeat certain words (there would be no commitment to the magnificent wings or even to any gleaming figure). Extreme literalists are those who insist that *all* of the doctrinal statements associated with their religion be read with the *maximal amount* of specificity—and for them, the warfare between science and religion is typically real and intense. For many others, however, the idea of a single doctrinal profile is clearly fanciful: when pressed, they feel unsure exactly how much of the everyday implications they want to import into the credal avowals that are most significant for them. Confessing to doctrinal indefiniteness, they resist producing clear and unambiguous translations of statements that play a central role in their lives.

To unsympathetic outsiders, doctrinal indefiniteness, or even the milder practice of retreating from the everyday implications of the language used in formulating religious claims, can appear evasive. Critics who detect a contradiction within the body of religious doctrine, or between articles of doctrine and well-confirmed results of inquiry, are informed that the apparent inconsistency is the product of simplistic reading, or worse that the exact content of the doctrine resists specification. Insistence on providing definite content for doctrinal statements ignores the long history of subtle interpretive strategies for reading the scriptures, as well as the more obvious point that the main religious texts were not written by people intending to submit articles to a modern scientific journal. Flexibility of interpretation is nonetheless easily abused, allowing retreat in response to criticism and a compensatory advance later, in exhortations to an audience of the faithful.

How, then, in such murky waters can secular humanism follow any clear current? By permitting many questions to go unanswered, but demanding a reply to one. The core of secularist doubt is skepticism about anything "transcendent." Believers may retreat from committing themselves to all-powerful creators with long white beards or to gleaming figures with magnificent wings or to the living physical presence of someone who was previously fully medically dead, but so long as they interpret their doctrines as recording episodes that were connected with something beyond the physical, organic, human world, secular humanists doubt the truth of what is claimed. Only when the believer is prepared to declare forthrightly that the resurrection is a metaphor to convey an important ideal—stating, perhaps, that when the man we know as Jesus died permanently, there was no abrogation of normal physical and organic processes, but that his acceptance of injustice and agonizing punishment reveals the wonderful human possibility of self-sacrifice—will the secularist conclude that nothing is left to provoke resistance. Strategies of interpretation may vary, doctrines may be admitted to be indefinite, but one question must be addressed: Does this doctrine presuppose some claim about something transcendent?

So far, I have only attempted to become clear about the character of secular humanist doubt. Let's now turn to the grounds for skepticism.

III

Many religions that once pervaded human societies have surely vanished without trace, but even when attention is focused on those known from ethnographic studies and from the historical record, we find an astounding variety in religious doctrines. Impersonal forces, sacred places, ancestors, ghosts, spirits, demons, and a wide diversity of deities have all figured as supposed manifestations of the transcendent. Sometimes religious cultures are aware of part of this variety, allowing tolerantly (as the Romans tended to do) that the divinities of the neighbors are, although inferior, fully real; sometimes they assert a more aggressive exclusivity: ours is the true religion, all the rest is primitive superstition. Assuming, for the moment, that the doctrines are understood with relative specificity, so that distinct religions give very different descriptions of the transcendent realm, an obvious question arises. How is it possible to make sense of this diversity of religious doctrine?

Even when religions make no explicit claim to exclusivity, it would strain credulity to admit all of the rival accounts as true. Nobody thinks the world is so full of mystic forces, sacred places, spirits, and divinities that the entire population of claimants can be accommodated. So long, then, as the interpretation of religious doctrine is sufficiently specific, literal enough to assert the existence of personal and impersonal beings, a distinction must be drawn between those religions that have an approximately accurate inventory and those that are utterly mistaken. Yet the bases of belief are remarkably similar across the entire array of religious traditions, including those condescendingly characterized as benighted superstitions. Leaving what are taken to be religious experiences on one side for the moment, the religious convictions of many contemporary believers are formed in very much the same ways. Often the faithful are born into a religious tradition whose lore they absorb in early childhood and continue to accept throughout their lives; sometimes, when the surrounding society contains adherents of a different doctrine, acquaintance with a rival religion prompts conversion, and a shift of allegiance. In either case, however, religious believers rely on a tradition they take to have carefully preserved insights once vouchsafed to privileged witnesses in a remote past. Because that pattern is so prevalent in undergirding the religious beliefs of the present, it is very hard to declare that one of the traditions has a special status, or even that a manageable few have transmitted truth about the transcendent. The beliefs of each tradition stand on much the same footing: complete symmetry prevails.

How can a devout person, deeply convinced of some specific, substantive doctrine—the claim that the world is the creation of a single personal deity, say—come to terms with this predicament? To face it clearly is to recognize that if, by some accident of early childhood, he had been transported to some distant culture, brought up among aboriginal Australians, for example, he would now affirm a radically different set of doctrines, perhaps about the reverberations of the Dreamtime in the present, and would do so with the same deep conviction and as a result of the same types of processes that characterize his actual beliefs. Insisting that his reading of the favored scriptures is accompanied by some special feeling, a *"sensu divinitatis,"* is fruitless, a fig-leaf covering for dogmatism. His Australian counterpart would avow similar feelings, aroused by listening to narratives about the sacred places, although he would not decorate his own professions with a Latin tag.

Confronted with this challenge, thoughtful religious people incline to one of two strategies (or sometimes opt for both). Symmetry is supposed to be broken either by the fact that some religions—the more "advanced" ones—come with an arsenal of theological weapons that can be used to repel doubt, or through the recognition that, beyond the familiar ways in which people can acquire new information—perception, memory, and the like—there are reliable means of gaining basic *religious* knowledge.

Appeals to the justifying power of rational theology propose an analogy between the judgments of scientists about the natural world and those of sophisticated theologians about the transcendent. Different cultures adopt alternative views of the same natural phenomena, about the facts of biological heredity for instance, but the diversity of belief doesn't provoke doubts about well-entrenched parts of science like molecular genetics. By the same token, the believer contends, the conclusions of intellectually well articulated religions can be differentiated from the religious ideas of cultures that have not yet developed rigorous ways of fathoming the transcendent.

The analogy not only divides the "advanced" religions from their "primitive" counterparts, but also fragments the community of those who profess a sophisticated religion, separating a tiny group of intellectuals who bestow religious enlightenment on the unwashed mass of the faithful. Does that image correspond to the self-understanding of the devout? Can it be reconciled with doctrines that the truth about the transcendent is available to all? Yet worse is to come. For, although diversity decreases when you suppose that only religions with a well-articulated intellectual tradition can acquire doctrinal truth, enough differences remain to revive the problem of symmetry. Christian theology is developed differently by different denominations, Islam and Judaism have their own constellations of alternative versions of rational doctrine, and beyond them lie the even more distinctive and diverse accounts provided by the many sects of Hinduism, of Buddhism, and of other Eastern religions. Disagreement in doctrine is mirrored in disagreement about cogent modes of religious argument. Finally, a closer look at the motivating analogy shows it to be broken-backed. In the scientific case, the methods used to generate and defend the conclusions can be tested independently for their reliability, and the conclusions themselves can be put to work in a host of successful predictions and interventions. Molecular geneticists can do remarkable things on an impressive scale, producing organisms to order and using them to manufacture a host of medically valuable substances (for example, growth hormones, clotting factors, or insulin). Nothing like that is apparent in even the longest-surviving traditions of rational religion. Instead arguments about the transcendent, including those directed at establishing the existence of a deity, are presented, rebutted, refined, and questioned again, in a process that makes no progress, in which no question is ever settled, in which opinion never converges and disagreement never abates. No basis can be found for supposing that this process is well suited to lead to transcendent truth. It seems to continue (indefinitely?) only because those committed to pursuing it already believe, on independent grounds, the doctrines of their favored tradition. Small wonder, then, that in many schools of rational religion, the official point of the enterprise is not to produce "proofs" to confound the unbeliever, but the more modest goal of elaborating a religious vision whose real sources lie elsewhere.

The second strategy invokes a power of basic knowledge, supposedly available to all, and thereby avoids splitting the body of the faithful into a discerning elite and the (gratefully?) enlightened laity. Yet why should anyone, including the religious believer, suppose himself to have an ability to undergo processes that yield specific doctrines about the transcendent? With respect to faculties like perception and memory, physics, physiology, and psychology have begun to provide the rudiments of accounts of our capacities to discern particular types of facts: we now have glimmerings of understanding as to how people have causal access to specific features of the world. For the putative source of transcendent truth there is nothing similar—and yet it would be quite reasonable for the religious believer to point out that, for most of human history, people have trusted their senses and their memories without having any adequate explanations of how these faculties might yield knowledge. Nevertheless, however flawed historical theorizing about sight and hearing and recollection has been, our ancestors have been able to base their trust on common-sense discoveries. They could check that, for the most part, the deliverances of the senses cohere, that the properties discerned by vision are reconfirmed by touch, that the judgments of different people agree and that a mass of perceptual judgments and memories fit together in a harmonious whole. Beyond that, they appreciated how things can go wrong, how dim light interferes with vision, how our abilities are weakened when we are tired or intoxicated, and they were able to use these fragments of everyday lore to make sense of disagreements. Indeed, even quite rudimentary pieces of mundane knowledge have helped people become *better* at observing and remembering.

If the appeal to a source of basic religious knowledge is to answer the challenge posed by symmetry, it must vindicate belief in particular substantive doctrines as privileged. The Christian *knows* that Christ was the son of God: but the Muslim who denies this and the Hindu who asserts the divinity of Vishnu are both deceived. How exactly is the difference to be explained? To suppose that reading the Christian gospels is like perceiving the surrounding environment in a clear light not only offers an utterly mysterious analogy, but also begs the crucial question. Muslims and Hindus may, with equal justice, contend that *their* favored scriptures are the media of enlightenment. No available pieces of everyday lore enable anyone to test the rival claims and thus adjudicate the dispute. We are left with the original gesture at a *sensu divinitatis*, and with dogmatism under a nicer name.

Appeals to previously unaccepted sources of "basic knowledge" are not the province of religion alone. Throughout human history, people have often supposed themselves equipped to extend their knowledge in special ways. Belief in the predictive power of dreams has been perennially popular, dissolving only under a track record of disagreement and disappointment, and with the failure of attempts to separate the expert prognosticators from the pretenders. Although the appeal to basic religious knowledge avoids the outright rebuke of definite refutation—for, unlike nature, the transcendent never delivers a resounding "No" to our assertions—it is undermined by the vast extent of radical disagreement, and by inability to explain in any noncircular way how the supposedly benighted might deploy their supposed faculties better than they actually manage. The problem of symmetry remains unsolved.

Defenders of specific religious doctrines can rightly object at this point that the deck has been stacked against them, through the deliberate neglect of an important part of the basis for belief, to wit the religious experiences believers sometimes have. Throughout history, people have reported episodes in which they have taken themselves to gain access to the transcendent, although how frequently such episodes occur is hard to assess, since the available statistics show wild variations in different years. Religious experiences occur in all cultures, and are invariably described using the categories either of a religion to which the subject already adheres or of a religion with which she is familiar. Once again, symmetry prevails. Moreover, cultures are typically sensitive to the possibility that those who report religious experiences have been deceived or even seduced into wick-edness, and they introduce special procedures for validating claims to encounter the transcendent, requiring that the messages allegedly delivered should conform to the orthodoxy handed down across the generations—as, for example, in the medieval certification of ancho-rites. Instead of serving as an independent source of justification for religious doctrine, religious experience is thus parasitic on the deliv-erances of tradition. The conclusions often taken to be grounded in religious experience are thoroughly soaked in the brew of doctrines prevalent in the surrounding society and typically passed on in early enculturation—an important fact neglected by individualistically oriented religious (usually Christian) epistemologists in their at-tempts to validate "basic religious knowledge."

My focus so far has been on commitments to specific religious doctrines. I have not considered the more plausible position that rational argument or a capacity for "basic knowledge" or a distinctive type of religious experience can achieve something less ambitious, warranting some conclusion that all religions, or all religions of some privileged type, share—for example, the claim that there is something transcendent; examining that suggestion will come later. I have ar-gued that not all of the full array of specific doctrines about the tran-scendent can be accepted as true—indeed, the overwhelming major-ity of them must be regarded as thoroughly false. Nevertheless, the processes through which those doctrines have come to be adopted are all of the same general type, providing no basis for distinguishing the wheat from the chaff. Under these circumstances, we should be skeptical about all of them.

The conclusion is reinforced by two centuries of careful investi-gation of religious traditions and their evolution. Scholars have traced the ways in which the scriptural canon has been assembled, showing how incompatible conceptions of what are supposedly the same transcendent phenomena and of the same historical events have been fused, presumably in an effort to incorporate distinctive ideas favored by different groups within a shared religious perspective. Careful research has demonstrated how doctrine has shifted to respond to the felt needs or aspirations of potential converts and how it has adapted to the political pressures of the moment—Mark's contorted account of the role of the Jews in demanding that Jesus be subjected to a Roman punishment is a case in point, a fiction that has caused destructive prejudice and extraordinary harm, but that surely eased the passage of nascent Christianity in a Rome-dominated world. Sociologists have studied how contemporary religions accommodate the psychological needs of those they hope to recruit, and how the accommodations modify the orthodox interpretations of religious claims and the emphasis placed on particular texts: the megachurches of the wealthy suburbs don't usually urge the centrality to Christianity of the Sermon on the Mount. Although the psychological study of religious experience is handicapped by recent sensitivities about the legitimacy of controlled experiments—it is no longer considered acceptable to administer psychotropic drugs to unwitting subjects in the hope of identifying an increased frequency in reports of encounters with the transcendent—the available evidence amply supports the hypothesis that religious experiences are more likely to happen to people who are psychologically disturbed or who are under the influence of substances usually viewed as interfering with clear and reliable perception.

The moral of these studies is that the routes to contemporary acceptance of religious doctrines are not merely of the same generic type, across societies and cultures, but that the historical genesis of belief is pervaded, if not entirely dominated, by processes of kinds quite unlikely to yield correct beliefs. Shaping ideas about the transcendent to evade political pressures or to accommodate the wishes of hoped-for converts is not a reliable means of generating true doctrines, or even of better approximating the truth. Simply absorbing the reports of religious experience provided by all and sundry would infect doctrine with all manner of delusions—which is surely why successful traditions have insisted on conformity to orthodoxy, and why many subjects of religious experience, the Prophet prominent among them, have worried about the genuineness of their voices and visions.

Most specific religious doctrines must be false, and since all emerge from the same generic style of historical development, it follows that generating belief in that way is not reliable. Two centuries' worth of studies—literary, historical, sociological, political, and anthropological—add an explanation of the unreliability. By doing so, they deepen the case for doubt.

IV

That case, as so far presented, faces obvious rejoinders, none perhaps more natural than the accusation of distorting the religious perspective by emphasizing knowledge and ignoring faith. "What exactly has been shown?" a critic may ask. "Merely that specific religious doctrines are not held as items of knowledge, or perhaps more precisely, not held as items of the mundane kind of knowledge that requires reliable ways of generating and sustaining belief. Thoughtful religious people should have been ready to concede as much from the beginning. They should have insisted that religious doctrines are held on the basis of faith, and, if it is apt to see them also as knowledge, then the knowledge is of a distinctive sort."

Yet the ground on which my imagined critic invites us to tread is slippery, and we should go slowly. First, is there religious knowledge? Some prominent religious traditions appear to claim it. In one of Handel's settings (from the third part of *Messiah*), the soprano sings gloriously of her knowledge of the living redeemer. If that knowledge is of some special type, an explanation is needed to show the kinship with the everyday conception—otherwise talk of knowledge will just be a misleading pun.

More importantly, the notion of faith deployed in major contemporary religions is many-sided. Faith can be constituted by trust in a person, or in some supposed embodiment of the transcendent; it can consist in commitment to an ideal or to living in a particular way. If, however, the issue concerns the acceptance of specific religious doctrines, the most straightforward sense involves a contrast with belief on the basis of evidence. In the uncharitable quip, faith is when you believe and you know it ain't so. On a slightly more sympathetic reading, faith is belief that outruns the evidence available to the believer. According to some religious people, even if religious doctrines are held without compelling evidence, such belief is legitimate.

What standard of legitimacy is at issue here? Surely not an *epistemic* one: we aren't dealing with *reasonableness* in Hume's sense when he declares that reasonable people proportion their beliefs to the evidence. To confute religious faith by declaring that legitimate beliefs are *defined* as those based on the available evidence would be silly, a glorious victory only for Humpty Dumpty. Fans of faith often hope to set human practices of forming belief within a broader context, one in which many different types of values come into play, and to regard a leap beyond the evidence as permissible in light of the entire spectrum of those values, or, at least, of the most important ones. The legitimacy at stake is ethical.

William James's "delicious *enfant terrible*," W. K. Clifford, denied any such legitimacy, arguing that "it is wrong, always, everywhere, and for anyone to believe anything on the basis of insufficient evidence," thereby provoking James to compose what is probably the most influential article ever written by an American philosopher. Clifford defended his sweeping generalization by considering scenarios in which believing beyond the evidence leads to actions causing great harm or the risk of such harm: his primary example is that of a ship owner who suppresses legitimate concerns about the seaworthiness of a vessel, and sends passengers and crew off to watery deaths. James replies by considering different scenarios, cases in which abstaining from belief would forfeit valuable consequences for the believer, and in which the impact on the welfare of others can be assumed to be negligible. A solitary mountaineer wills himself into believing that a difficult leap will succeed—and lands safely in virtue of his conviction. A suitor courts his beloved with unwarranted confidence, and thereby increases his chances of winning her. Neither inflicts damage on anyone else. Secularists can concede the validity of these examples, abandon Clifford's ambitious principle, and yet deny the ethical permissibility of holding religious doctrines by a "leap of faith." Precisely because religious commitments typically pervade the lives of the devout, they are not insulated from actions with serious consequences for others. As the most vocal contemporary atheists rightly recognize, to believe in earnest is a spur to proselytizing, to efforts at persuasion, even to coercion, punishment, and campaigns to eradicate the party of evil. Only if the tie between belief and action were completely cut, or if conduct were under the firm control of an internal censor, dedicated to ensuring that only ethically permissible actions are performed, could the adoption of specific doctrine on the basis of faith be legitimate. In the former instance, what the believer declares in her heart would never be expressed in her conduct, leaving a faith so attenuated as to be scarcely worthy of the name; in the latter, the primary religious commitment is to orient life by recognizing important values, and belief in doctrine figures only as a means to realizing ends of intrinsic worth; faith is ethically legitimate because it is focused on the ethical.

Viewing faith as a commitment to fundamental ethical ideals is the most direct way of responding to Clifford's critique, but it is at odds with Kierkegaard's provocative attempt to understand and to celebrate religious faith. Abraham, the "knight of faith," is prepared to sacrifice his son, Isaac, to fulfill a divine command, in full awareness of his ethical obligation to protect the boy, in full consciousness of his love for Isaac, and in full recognition that the sacrifice will apparently nullify God's promise to him that his descendants will "cover the earth." He believes not only on "insufficient evidence," but also knowing that the combination of his convictions is paradoxical—he believes "in virtue of the absurd." While admitting that he does not understand Abraham, Kierkegaard admires him, precisely because of his willingness to "suspend the ethical" and to honor the absolute duty to God.

Any temptation to discern some overriding value in Abraham's devotion to the deity should be scotched by the realization that what he is prepared to do would deprive his son of any similar opportunity: the "nobility" of being the "knight of faith" is purchased for himself by denying the possibility to Isaac. Abraham stands at the end of a continuum of those who are ready to do profoundly inhumane things in the name of religious faith, a continuum whose other, milder pole is occupied by the irresponsible believers who troubled Clifford. Giving a general license to commitments to religious doctrines that outrun the evidence allows the members of the diverse array of human cultures and societies to act on the basis of whatever interpretation they give to whatever sayings or texts they choose, to permit their inspiration to be *Mein Kampf* or the *120 Days of Sodom*, and that is to tolerate fanaticism in all its guises. Unless the application of doctrine is always subordinated to a commitment to ethical values, unless there is *no* "suspension of the ethical," the invocation of faith cannot legitimize acceptance of religious doctrine.

V

Let us take stock. Secularist doubt is prompted by probing the processes that generate specific beliefs about the transcendent. Those processes are so unreliable that all of the conflicting specific religious doctrines are, almost certainly, false. Nor can adherence to such doctrines be condoned by supposing that believers exercise an ethically permissible expression of faith.

Nonetheless, secularists need not categorically deny the possibility of the transcendent. They ought to be mindful of the history of inquiries into the natural world. Scientists have often been confident that major features of nature have been finally determined, only to learn that radical revision is in order. The history of human knowledge has been marked by recurrent surprises—the world has often turned out to be richer and stranger than had previously been suspected. Secularists cannot rule out the possibility that, someday, the future march of rigorous inquiry, applying and refining the canons of careful reasoning developed not only in the natural sciences but in all the disciplines, from anthropology and art history at the beginning of the alphabet to zoology at the end, will disclose an aspect of reality apparently dimly prefigured in some religious doctrines, inspiring the retrospective judgment "So *that's* what the world's religions were trying to gesture at all along!"

But how could that happen? On some understandings of the vague term 'transcendent,' the transcendent is inaccessible to the methods of everyday inquiry. To make sense of the scenario, we have to suppose that some future extension of those methods, recognized as reliable, is employed to disclose a type of entity so remarkable and so different from other aspects of reality that it inspires conceptual revision. The new disclosure seems to reveal what the various religions, in their confused and inchoate ways, had been pointing toward, prompting a weaker notion of the transcendent that retains the idea of something quite different from mundane reality but allows the possibility of detection by the newest reliable modes of investigation. Attempts to envisage the details of the discovery defeat the imagination: at best, we can entertain the outline thought of our successors reaching reasoned agreement on the existence of something deep about the universe, something they can connect to major articles of religious doctrine. We have only inklings of a possibility. Yet that bare possibility should be admitted.

Conceding that much leaves the heart of the secular critique untouched. Contemporary people have not lived through the hypothetical transition, and, from where we stand, there is good evidence for skepticism about all extant specific doctrines regarding the transcendent, and no evidence to suggest the reality of the transcendent in any form. To the extent that we can make educated guesses at the future of rigorous inquiry, as investigators continue to deploy and refine reliable methods of assessing evidence, the judgment does not change. From our present perspective, acceptance of the transcendent is a wild leap: belief is simply speculative conjecture.

Religious believers may protest that this verdict ignores a more sophisticated use of ideas that were broached earlier. Instead of thinking of rational theology or basic religious knowledge or religious experience as justifying specific religious doctrines, believers may make a more modest claim: one (or more) of these provides evidence, here and now, for the existence of the transcendent. Modesty abandons the ambitious enterprise of vindicating some particular religion—and thereby sidesteps the problems of adjudicating the clash of specific doctrines. Nevertheless, although the modest approach is *more* plausible, it inherits a crucial problem posed by the secularist case.

Fans of rational theology often propose that the physical existence of the cosmos can only—*"ultimately"*—be explained by supposing a creative intelligence behind it; those who feel a *sensu divinitatis* believe it to warrant (at least) the existence of a transcendent realm; religious experience may not justify doctrines about specific deities, but, some suppose, it is a window into a world beyond. In all three proposals, however, proper evidential standards are modified. Rigorous inquiry sometimes introduces new entities into our picture of the universe by showing how those entities would help explain previously puzzling phenomena. Although the canons of good explanation are various, none of them sanction the idea of a transcendent creative mind as an explanatory hypothesis. Similarly, none of the standards for appraising evidential connections between believers and the world, deployed in evaluating claims to basic knowledge or forms of experience, would validate theses that vaguely characterized psychological states in religious subjects stand in an evidential relation to an equally vaguely described transcendent. In all three instances, whatever superficial attractions the proposals have—and even whatever definite *content* they have—is derivative from specific religious traditions. The thought of *evidence* for the transcendent is parasitic on those traditions, generated by tacitly presupposing a particular religious perspective that gives substance to the claim to know. Detached from its moorings, in efforts to sidestep the problems posed by doctrinal conflict, it floats free, contentless and unwarranted.

Unless "evidence" is to be used in a radically new (and unspecified) sense, there is no present evidence for the transcendent. Yet religious sympathizers, inspired by the possibility that the transcendent may one day be disclosed to us, may offer an even more modest proposal. Although we have grounds for one type of doubt about the transcendent (since we lack evidence for it), we should not proceed to the stronger species of doubt that consists in active disbelief. The proper secularist attitude is agnosticism. Recognizing that the future might reveal the existence of something our descendants would connect with doctrines of major religions, we should hold ourselves open to that possibility. Maintaining that openness is both legitimate and important.

Inquiry, even at its most rigorous, is fallible. Future generations may revise claims we take to be firmly established. Does that imply that we should be tentative about everything? Surely not. We rightly take seriously those results of previous inquiries that rest on compelling evidence, using them to guide our actions, even when the costs of going wrong would be severe. Despite what we now believe, it may turn out that along with their physical constituents living things contain a vital force, or that the ghosts of the departed return to their old habitations, or that the world has sixty-seven dimensions (to choose a number at random). There is little temptation to think we should be especially open-minded about these possibilities, or that we should not proceed to active disbelief. Why is the case of the transcendent any different? Is it perhaps because a cousin of a famous argument of Pascal's lurks in the background? Discovery of the transcendent would be so wonderful, transforming the human condition, and hence this particular possibility should inspire agnosticism rather than blunt denial. If that is the motivation, it is seriously deficient. For not only do we currently have no evidence for the existence of the transcendent, but we also lack any basis for conjectures about the consequences of any hypothetical discovery of it. Only a tacit reliance on the specific doctrines of traditional religions prompts the judgment that discovering something we came to see as answering to a revised notion of the transcendent would be especially rewarding. Since we have grounds for thinking those doctrines to be almost certainly false, there's no reason to suppose the transformative power of this discovery would be any greater than that of identifying vital forces, returning ghosts, or even a sixty-seven-dimensional universe.

Historical studies sometimes show how surprising developments in the sciences recapitulate the dim and inchoate suggestions of much earlier thinkers, whose ideas have been treated as marginal (at best). Ancient conjectures about indivisible parts of matter were revived in nineteenth-century atomic chemistry; thinkers who lived long before Darwin speculated about the evolution of life. By analogy with these historical precedents, if some notion of a transcendent realm is rehabilitated, we can expect it to exceed the conceptual grasp of its earlier champions. Barring extraordinary luck, specific religious doctrines will be revealed as thoroughly erroneous, and indeed as framed in entirely inadequate language. Even if the day of discovery dawns, it is overwhelmingly unlikely to vindicate the Dreamtime or the transmigration of souls, the Hindu pantheon or the Trinity, even the thought of a divine creator or of a mind behind the universe. All the categories religions have deployed are, almost certainly, inadequate to their intended task.

Pursuit of doubt leads secular humanism to a position rarely made explicit: "soft atheism," as I shall call it. Soft atheism makes small concessions in the direction of agnosticism: while there is no basis for endorsing the transcendent, the bare possibility of some future justified acceptance cannot be eliminated. In the interim, we have no reason to treat the existence of a transcendent realm as a serious possibility, one more deserving open-mindedness than a myriad other potential revisions of currently well-established beliefs. With respect to the substantive doctrines of the world's religions, soft atheists are as firm as their harder cousins: there are excellent grounds for supposing all such doctrines to be thoroughly false.

VI

The most prominent contemporary critiques of religion prompt many believers to reply that they do not touch the *real* faith, the form of devotion espoused by the most thoughtful and sensitive adherents. Critics are accused of oversimplifying, of substituting crude caricatures for complex commitments, of assimilating all religion to fundamentalism. The accusations have some merit, in that many contemporary articulations of atheism presuppose that religious doctrines are to be read with considerable specificity, although whether the level of specificity assumed assimilates all religion to fundamentalism is a separate issue, one probably answered differently in different cases. Yet to dismiss atheist critiques as substituting caricatures for finely shaded portraits overlooks the obvious fact that, however subtle the religious conceptions of those who inhabit divinity schools or faculties of religion, of those who write books—or book reviews—about religious questions, many believers would acquiesce in the interpretive approaches assumed by the critics, reading religious doctrines just as they do. Indeed, the fastest growing religions, in many parts of the world, are those insisting on substantive doctrines construed with considerable specificity (religions in the neighborhood of the "literalist" pole). The "real faith" may be untouched by the standard objections of contemporary atheist broadsides, it may have been articulated and defended for centuries by the most intelligent and subtle religious thinkers, but it is hardly the form of religion that is most vital, and sometimes most violent, in the modern world.

My skeptical argument, too, does not target all forms of religion. Indeed, it has been marked by periodic assumptions, indicating places at which alternative conceptions of religion might be developed. *Assuming* first that religions are centered on doctrines, second that doctrines are read by importing the specific implications of the words used to formulate them, and third that faith is not viewed as a commitment to ethical values and ideals, my secularist argument generates its soft atheist conclusion. When these assumptions are suspended, however, it is possible to recognize an alternative version of religion— and alternative versions of the major world religions—that evade the reasoning. Moreover, this rival conception allows for an elaboration of the religious challenge to secular humanism, with which this chapter began. It thus enables important issues to be joined.

Chapter 3 will consider a more refined version of religion. Because the account I propose depends on talk of values, I first need to explain how a secularist perspective can make sense of such talk. Providing that explanation, the task of the next chapter, already begins to address the religious challenge. I shall try to show how secularists can obtain a clearer and more convincing account of ethical values than anything religion, in any of its traditional forms, can provide.

TWO

VALUES VINDICATED

I

Ivan Karamazov is only the most famous of those who believe that, in the absence of God, everything is permitted. Many people take it for granted that ethics is a province of religion: divine commands, and only divine commands, could serve as the foundation for binding prescriptions on human lives and human conduct. Yet this general approach to ethical life has been in trouble ever since Plato's Socrates posed a dilemma for Euthyphro: if goodness is what the deity wills, does the goodness arise from the divine willing, or does the willing respond to the goodness? In the first case, the source of goodness is an arbitrary fiat; in the second, there is a source of goodness prior to and independent of the deity's will.

The dilemma serves to pose a puzzle: appreciating the force of Socrates' argument is not difficult; why, then, is the idea of a tight link between religion and ethics so perennially popular? The answer, I suggest, lies in the difficulty of producing any persuasive rival account of ethics—and of values generally—that will not reduce ethical life to the expression of subjective attitudes. Abandon the religious foundation and, it seems, the concepts of ethical demands and prohibitions and permissions lose their objective force. Ivan

Karamazov was not quite accurate in his formulation, but it is easy to recognize what his creator had in mind.

I shall try to show how we can escape from this intellectual predicament. A brief sketch of the ethical life will prepare the way for a more precise understanding of the problem.

Fully ethical beings are those able to direct their conduct by judgments about what they believe to be good or right or virtuous or valuable. Although most of their lives may be led by expressing entrenched habits, there are occasions on which they stop, consider what course of action would be best, and proceed on the basis of their deliberations. They can subordinate some of their wishes, even their most intense impulses, to the value judgments they accept. They can reflect on those value judgments and discuss them with their fellows. They can ponder potential techniques for giving their considered evaluations more power to govern their actions. So the fully ethical life requires a complex array of psychological dispositions and capacities. Some of its elements are occasionally visible among non-human animals that act in ways that appear praiseworthy. Our evolutionary cousins sometimes respond to the needs of their fellows; on other occasions they appear to suppress strong desires because of their expectations about the consequences of pursuing what they dearly want. But the only fully ethical beings we know of are human.

Many people take the ethical life to be answerable to an objective standard, "external" in the sense that it is prior to and independent of human choices and decisions. Those who stop to think about how to respond to their situation may try their best to find the right continuation, but ethical success is not guaranteed, not even if their conclusion is thoroughly endorsed by the settled judgments of their society. As already noted, the most popular view locates the external standard in the transcendent realm. On some philosophical accounts too, the standard is divorced from the natural world, grounded in a domain of Platonic forms or non-natural properties. On one reading of Kant, adopted by some of his followers, the standard is displaced from the transcendent, locating the "moral law within"—"internal" in a sense, but "external" in being independent of our feelings and preferences; ethical principles are *discovered*, not *constructed* by us. (As we shall see, there is an alternative interpretation and a rival tradition that emphasizes "Kantian constructivism.") According to accounts of this sort, the external standard is constituted by idealized processes of practical reason, denizens of a "realm of reason" to be separated from the natural world.

Other philosophers resist the divorce between the ethical and the physical, organic, social world. They seek to explain the standard in completely natural terms. The good is measured by the aggregate of pleasure over pain across the class of sentient beings. Or value properties are dispositions to induce emotional reactions. Or (a particularly inadequate proposal) goodness is calculated in the fundamental currency of Darwinian evolution, reproductive success.

An important challenge to secular humanism charges that any satisfactory account of the ethical life must appeal to an external standard and that it is impossible to do so without recourse to the transcendent. Plainly, the form of the challenge suggests two different lines of reply. One attempts to dispense with any external standard: ethical deliberations answer only to the local ethical code. Disaster seems to threaten that strategy, for it gives up any touchstone for assessing the rival codes of different societies. As the religious challenger predicted, the destined route seems to lead to Ivan Karamazov. On the other hand, efforts at identifying a natural basis for values suffer from a host of familiar objections. The would-be identifications fail to pick out the correct classes of actions as good or bad, valuable or worthless, and, as a host of critics and commentators have contended, they fail to explain the force ethical judgments exercise upon those who adopt them. So the prospects for a naturalistic account of the external standard do not seem bright.

We are left, then, with a contest between the religious anchoring of values in the transcendent, and a cluster of philosophical accounts that divorce the standard from the natural world. Not only do the philosophical alternatives appear abstruse and nebulous, by contrast with the more familiar idea of a divine commander, but they also have difficulty making sense of moments of ethical discovery. How should we explain those episodes in which ethical advances seem to occur— for example, when people came to recognize the wrongness of slavery? Can we credit the innovators with some hitherto unprecedented access to non-natural properties or a new ability to appreciate the demands of practical reason? For that matter, could we find any *natural* facts they detected for the first time, facts overlooked by their contemporaries who resisted their proposals? To understand a scientific discovery it is necessary to appreciate the altered cognitive relations between discoverers and the aspects of nature they disclose: you can't explain the discovery of X-rays without presenting Röntgen's connection to a new type of radiation, or the discovery of the laws of inheritance without showing how Mendel obtained indirect access to the genes of the pea plants he bred. Historical accounts of the origins of the abolitionist movement make no mention of any of the philosophical candidates for the external standard to which ethical life answers. They do, however, spend considerable time in reviewing the religious debates about the legitimacy of slavery—and taking those debates to be central to the discovery sits comfortably with the thought that ethical advances are fueled by a renewal of divine illumination.

Despite the force of Socrates' dilemma, the tight connection between religion and ethics survives. Nobody has succeeded in formulating any rival account of ethics that is both readily comprehensible and widely persuasive. Unless the trouble stems from people's difficulties in understanding the abstractions of philosophy, we might echo Churchill's famous judgment about democracy: the idea of a religious foundation for ethics is the worst available theory of the ethical life—except for all of its rivals.

How, then, to meet the religious challenge—or, more generally, how to account for the apparent objectivity of ethics? We need a new framework, one that expands the range of options apparently available. A broader perspective can emerge if we follow Darwin's most fundamental insight: when we are puzzled about some cluster of phenomena we can sometimes liberate ourselves from a restricted range of apparent possibilities by taking a historical approach, and asking how those phenomena have come to be. The full ethical life requires a complex set of conditions. Tracing their emergence—or more exactly, sometimes seeing how changes actually occurred, and settling for hypotheses about the possibility of negotiating transitions in cases where the evidence is incomplete or elusive—makes it possible to reconfigure questions of ethical objectivity, to escape from a menu of options limited by inadequate concepts. Developing the genealogy will take time, and objections are likely to flood in along the way. I hope that by the time the story is complete, I shall have assembled the resources for providing answers.

II

Human beings evolved from ancestors who had a few of the traits needed for full ethical life. Many primates have genetically encoded neurotransmitters inclining them to take pleasure in the company of their fellows, and it is overwhelmingly likely that sociality extends deep into the pre-human past. In our more recent history, since the time of our common ancestors with chimpanzees and bonobos (probably around seven million years ago), hominids have lived in social groups of a very particular sort: bands of about thirty to seventy conspecifics, mixed by age and sex. For all of its neural attractions, living together is not easy. Large numbers of primate species settle for more sporadic social interactions, or severely limit the number of mature males in the group, or opt for a smaller troop size. Like the chimpanzees and bonobos of today, our hominid ancestors managed a relatively complex and fluid set of social arrangements.

Their achievement rested on a psychological capacity recognizable in our evolutionary cousins, one that inspires some primatologists to identify the "building blocks of morality" in chimpanzees and bonobos, and, by extension, in the most recent ancestor we share with them. These animals have the ability to identify the wishes and intentions of their fellows and, consequent on the recognition, to adjust their own plans so as to aid others in reaching the attributed goals. The capacity, *responsiveness* to give it a name, promotes cooperative projects and accommodations that reduce social tension. Yet responsiveness is limited. The ally who helped yesterday proves indifferent today, and the lack of response arouses protest and conflict. Eventually reconciliation is needed, and the animals must huddle in close proximity, reassuring one another through mutual grooming.

The social life of chimpanzees, and even that of the more relaxed bonobos, is tense and fragile. Because these animals have a capacity for responsiveness, they can live together as they do; because that capacity is restricted they cannot live together easily. Time-and-motion experts would be appalled at the wastefulness of three hours spent in grooming on a normal day, and six hours dedicated to gestures of reassurance when the social order is threatened. Possibilities for profitable cooperative ventures go unrealized; group size is bounded by the daily demands for face-to-face interaction.

Human group size began to increase only in the late Paleolithic, fifteen thousand to twenty thousand years before the present, meaning that hundreds of thousands of generations of our hominid ancestors spent their lives in the same predicament. How, then, did our species escape? Perhaps through the acquisition of some mechanism for generating responses to others in particular contexts: a disposition to perceive the needs of the offspring of others and to assist in parental care, for example. What seems required, however, is something that could operate more generally, across a large range of everyday circumstances, a universal enhancement of responsiveness to those in the vicinity, not a purpose-built mechanism. Since widespread benevolence remains uncommon, it is more promising to look elsewhere.

Studies of chimpanzees reveal an ability to control pressing desires in the presence of an established social practice—as when members of the troop wait their turn for drinking water. Investigations of social primates, and of very young children, show a similar capacity for self-restraint in pairwise interactions, where there is an established pattern of mutual expectations. An obvious hypothesis is that our hominid ancestors further extended an incipient ability for self-control, so that their conduct became subject to *normative guidance*. From the initial perception of certain initially intended forms of behavior as generating unwelcome consequences, and from the awareness of expectations about actions in dyadic partnerships, they elaborated the practice of self-restraint across a widening set of circumstances. With the acquisition of language came the ability to represent the types of contexts and problematic actions, to specify patterns for conduct. Those specifications could be made not only—indeed, probably not primarily—by an individual agent to bind his own behavior, but also in discussion with others. Out of that discussion would come rules for action, patterns for life together, stories to make them vivid and effective, structures for a shared social life, passed on across the generations by methods for transmitting to the young the lore of the group.

If, as anthropologists suppose, the conditions of hominid social life were akin to those of contemporary hunter-gatherers (the surviving groups whose environments are closest to those of our ancestors), socially embedded normative guidance would be worked out among adult members of the groups on terms of rough equality. In challenging environments no mature individual is dispensable, and it would be risky not to allow all voices to be heard and not to seek an outcome all could accept. For tens of thousands of years, then, our human precursors, equipped with full language, formulated the codes that were to govern their lives together. They continued a project initiated at least fifty thousand years before the present, and possibly far older, perhaps begun by ethical pioneers whose linguistic skills were far more rudimentary. We are their heirs, and like them we continue the ethical project.

Ethics did not begin with the responsiveness of our remote primate ancestors, or with the exertion of self-control directed by the perception of mutual expectations in a dyadic interaction, or even with the earliest ventures in specifying the patterns of behavior to which group members would be expected to conform. The beginnings were almost certainly crude and simple: directives to share resources and to avoid unprovoked violence. Moreover, the most likely candidate for the emotion initially recruited to motivate conformity is fear: temptation to stray was quelled by the anticipation of punishment to follow. A practice focused on such primitive imperatives, in which compliance is the result of fear, seems unworthy to count as the start of ethics.

Socially embedded normative guidance set the stage for processes of cultural selection, in which elements of the codes tried out by different groups competed for transmission across space and time. Besides winnowing specific patterns of behavior, selection culled the techniques through which group members were brought to feel the force of the requirements the local code set down. Successful experiments built the human conscience, finding ways to internalize the preferred patterns of conduct, making the commanding voice seem as if it came from within, recruiting a wider repertoire of emotions to motivate the approved behavior. Human beings have acquired a heterogeneous assemblage of devices for redirecting their intentions, as the fear of punishment has been supplemented by respect for the group and its traditions, pride in alignment with the code and corresponding shame and guilt at lapses from it, solidarity with fellows and more besides. In the way of evolution generally, redundancy is valuable, allowing a system to be buffered against the failure of some key component. Perhaps we should be suspicious of the familiar philosophical idea of a special "ethical point of view," reached in the attainment of some distinctive process of reasoning or some privileged emotion. There may only be a hodge-podge of motivational devices, all of them welcome, none of them acquired at the moment when ethics "really" began. If the complex of elements that distinguish the ethical life was assembled gradually, it would be foolish to seek some non-arbitrary stage at which human beings—or hominids?—crossed a threshold and truly began the *ethical* project.

Skip forward. Among the first written documents that have been preserved, dating from roughly five thousand years ago, are addenda to bodies of law, testifying both to the complex forms of social organization attained in ancient Mesopotamia and to the pre-existence of systems of rules and patterns for behavior assembled over many generations. Cultural evolution must have led from the earliest ethical—or proto-ethical—practices, probably akin to the practices of contemporary hunter-gatherers, to the codes of the far larger groups who inhabited the first cities (approximately eight thousand years ago, thus three thousand years before the invention of writing). The clues from the Paleolithic are too scanty to discriminate among many possible ways in which the evolution of culture might have gone, but we can be confident about some of the steps that occurred. First, perhaps because of the need to increase the supply of scarce resources, some cultures adopted a division of labor. Efficiencies in apportioning tasks, as well as an increase in the number of cooperative activities, probably led to the generation of occasional surpluses, allowing for profitable exchanges with neighboring bands, and a concomitant expansion of the ethical framework to cover, at least in some contexts, people who had previously been regarded with suspicion or hostility and who had hitherto been outside the protections of the ethical code. Archaeologists have recognized evidence for trading networks twenty thousand years before the present, and by fifteen thousand to ten thousand years ago there are signs of temporary associations of different groups. The domestication of plants and animals (at the end of the same period) probably brought the institution of private property. Finally, the structuring of human life around cooperative interactions, often with the same partner, surely engendered an appreciation of the importance of mutual responsiveness. That was reflected in later ethical codes as a valuable ideal, something to be striven for and cherished independently of the ostensible goals of particular cooperative ventures. So arose the conception of enduring relationships as central to human life, and the far richer sense of the possibilities for human existence discernible in the early works of Western philosophy, and already glimpsed in Mesopotamian and Egyptian documents from earlier millennia. The ethical project has yielded a repertoire of emotions, desires, and ideals, unavailable to the early pioneers and beyond the scope of their imaginings.

Two additional aspects of the evolution of the project help in addressing the religious challenge. By the time of the settlement of the first cities, human societies had surely lost the egalitarian character of the origins. Private control of domesticated livestock probably played an important role in generating the later hierarchies of Ur and Babylon. Already in the division of labor and the differentiation of roles, a contrast among rival possibilities for the shape of human lives may have planted the seeds of future inequality.

Beyond these eroding tendencies, however, egalitarianism was challenged by a second cultural innovation. Ethnographic records testify to the popularity of a useful device for increasing compliance with a group's code when members are no longer in view of their fellows: invoke some instrument of detection, a transcendent policeman, a deity in the sky who observes all and is intent on punishing those who deviate. This idea was probably not the point of entry for religious doctrine; more likely it was grafted on to antecedent beliefs about a higher realm. But its advantages are evident, and it was surely widely borrowed or reinvented. Once the idea was in place, it disrupted the earlier equality in ethical discussion. People who could successfully convince others of their own access to the policeman's will now enjoyed the authority to declare the ways in which the prevalent code should be amended. Ethical insight became the province of a discerning few.

Religion long ago modified the character of ethical discussion by undermining the original egalitarianism. Allowing individuals to portray themselves as ethical authorities has sometimes, probably often, introduced idiosyncratic biases into ethical codes in the guise of expressions of the divine will. Yet recognizing these negative consequences should be balanced by appreciating the sometimes revolutionary power of religious formulations of ethical precepts. When the psalmist urges justice for the afflicted or the Jesus of the gospels commands love of our enemies, the ideal of responsiveness to others is radically extended. People typically excluded from the ethical conversation are given a presence and a voice. Religious authority is responsible not only for the inscription of prejudices—the prohibitions of Leviticus and the like—but also for some of the most powerful appreciations of our failures of responsiveness. Many resonant religious declarations echo in the ethical thought of contemporary secularists.

III

So far, a story—one that is short on many important details, probably mistaken about some others, but, with luck, a rough account of the route that has led to contemporary ethical life. Suppose, then, that something of this general sort is right. Can we talk of ethical truth and ethical falsehood, or envisage any objective standard according to which divergent ethical judgments might in principle be assessed?

When we look back into history, it is hard to resist such assessments. During the past four decades appraisal of sexual relationships has turned away from interest in the sexes of the partners or the organs brought into contact, to concentrate instead on more significant factors—whether the relationships are coercive or mutually fulfilling, enduring or ephemeral. From the late eighteenth century to the present, uneven and sporadic processes have modified the status of women, affording them greater opportunities. Chattel slavery is no longer viewed as permissible. Reaching further back into history, the ancient prescriptions of Mesopotamian law codes directing that the murder of a child should be avenged by killing the child of the perpetrator gave way, a millennium later, to the more familiar idea of exacting the murderer's own life (hardly the last word, but surely an improvement on the law it replaced). Even deeper in the past lies a Paleolithic transition in which some ethical precepts were extended to include, at least for a limited range of contexts, the members of a neighboring band.

Examples like these suggest that the history of ethical practice is not a sequence of *mere changes*, simply "one damned thing after another" bereft of any asymmetry to give it direction. Global judgments about progress may be problematic, comparisons of the culture of one society at one time with that of the same, or a different, society at a different time impossible. Ethical progress may be unsystematic and even rare. Nevertheless, with respect to a sample of episodes in which one pattern for conduct gave way to a different one, talk of progress appears irresistible. People who have lived through the transition are appalled by the thought that it would be equally justifiable to go back.

But is the concept of ethical progress coherent? Apparently, progress requires an external standard of ethical truth. The abolitionists recognized a truth—that slavery is wrong—at odds with the dominant judgment of their contemporaries that the "peculiar institution" was permissible (or, according to Cotton Mather in some moods, even ethically required). Yet history reveals no moment at which the relations between a pioneer abolitionist and the sources of ethical truth were modified; there seems to be no analogue of Röntgen's famous encounter with a fluorescing screen that sparked his discovery of X-rays or Mendel's observations of his pea plants, his tabulations of the frequencies of various characteristics and his analysis of the results. Historical analysis can present the circumstances under which early opponents of slavery—John Woolman, for example—first came to doubt the rightness of the prevailing attitudes, but it supplies no clues about the character of the shift in relations to external sources of truth that supposedly took place. As already noted, distinguished historians write compelling accounts of the change in attitude, without committing themselves to any views about the character of the external standard—or even providing any clues as to what it might be.

Religious people will see the inability to identify the newly detected "facts," whether they are assumed to be natural facts or whether they are the more esoteric elements proposed by philosophical theorizing, as the impoverished consequence of secularism. A secular genealogy of ethics inevitably debunks ethical practice, undermining any attempt to take even our most cherished values seriously. When progress occurs, as in the example of the abolition of slavery, what history reveals is a *religious* conversation. Yet here, I suggest, the emphasis is wrongly placed. The important achievement of the ethical revolutionaries is that they initiate a *conversation:* they re-create something akin to the early stages of the ethical project.

The source of the predicament in which secularists seem to be trapped is an inadequate conception of progress. Ethical progress is taken to consist in the discovery of some prior truth, and, in consequence, attempts to understand the historical episodes are driven by a quest for the moment at which the innovators apprehended the sources of the newly identified truth. But this is not the only possible perspective. Instead, progressive ethical change might consist in a collective construction of an amended ethical code. Out of the conversation initiated by the pioneers comes something new, something shaped by demands and needs that were previously unsatisfied, even unacknowledged. So far, that is just a gesture toward a rival perspective. To develop it more precisely, we should start by considering the varieties of progress.

Even in the case of the theoretical sciences, where notions of cognitive progress seem most at home, it is not uncontroversial that progress should be identified with the replacement of error by true belief. In other domains of human practice, in technology and in medicine, for example, progress is typically made through overcoming the problematic features of the current situation. Progress in transportation technology often consists in constructing new vehicles to break the barriers previously imposed on travel; progress in medicine is made by developing new techniques for curing, treating, or palliating conditions that were hitherto painful, disabling, or even fatal. New propositional knowledge sometimes serves as a means to progress in these areas, but it is not the heart of the matter.

With this in mind, recall the narrative of the early phases of the ethical project. Socially embedded normative guidance provided a way out of a problematic situation, whose symptoms were the recurrent instabilities of hominid and human social life, and whose underlying cause lay in our restricted responsiveness to one another. The deep feature of the human predicament is that evolution has bequeathed to us a disposition to live together, and a limited capacity for the necessary responsiveness to others—we can do it, but we cannot naturally do it easily or well. Ethics began by partially overcoming the problems posed by this predicament, introducing patterns and structures into our ancestors' social lives in compensation for their prevalent tendencies to fail to respond to one another. It started as a form of social technology.

Provided progress is viewed as problem solving, the concept of ethical progress proves coherent. All too frequently the understanding of progress is limited by thinking in terms of proximity toward some fixed goal: so cognitive progress is identified with approximation to the truth. Yet it would be absurd to envisage some ideal system of transportation, and to suppose that progress in this domain is constituted by realizing its features ever more closely, or to think of doctors as trying to help their patients approximate some ideal state of perfect health. Better to think in terms of "progress from" rather than "progress to"—and to make the same switch of perspective in the ethical case as well. Doing that entails abandoning a picture that has beguiled religious thinkers as well as secular philosophers, the vision of an antecedently fixed standard, an "ethical order of the cosmos," something we strive to discover and to exemplify in our lives and deeds. Instead, there is only the ongoing project, always beset by difficulties and never finished. It is a thoroughly human endeavor in which progress is made by solving problems. Understanding the project for what it is might enable us to solve those problems more systematically, and to do so at a higher rate.

The general predicament from which the ethical project tries to liberate us can always reemerge in new guises. Elaborating patterns of greater responsiveness requires balancing the claims of different individuals or groups in situations of conflict, and changing circumstances can call for review of balances already struck. Yet that is not the only source of new challenges. Technological solutions typically beget further problems. New vehicles, for example, require rules and structures for coordinating their movements, systems for enforcing the rules and maintaining the structures, methods of training users and provisions for dealing with occasions on which things go wrong—in the end, we need not only cars, but also roads and traffic signals and rules for driving and inspection of vehicles and traffic police and driver education and insurance and traffic courts . . . and on and on. A device, a type of vehicle or an ethical ideal, is introduced to address an existing problem, acquiring the function of solving that problem, but the solution is subject to particular conditions, posing the new problem of maintaining those conditions, and conferring a new function on the devices created to tackle that new problem. So new problems are born, and functions generate new functions. The original function of ethics was to overcome the limits of our responsiveness, but the evolution of the ethical project has brought new functions in its train.

When the demands imposed on satisfying one function do not interfere with the fulfillment of others, the task of the technologist is relatively straightforward: find a device that does everything. In practice, that may prove difficult, but when functions conflict, there is an additional issue to be resolved: given that addressing one problem requires sacrificing the thoroughness with which others can be overcome, how is an order of priorities to be established? Functional conflict makes difficulties for other forms of technology, and it is the root cause of why ethics is so hard.

The concept of progress so far on offer is thus incomplete. Because new problems emerge, functional conflict is a possibility, and when it arises there must be some specification of what compromises among functions are to constrain progressive change. A primary instance of functional conflict in the ethical case results from an important shift in ethical practice: the original function of ethics, overcoming the limits of our responsiveness to others, was initially fulfilled through normative discussions on terms of rough equality, but, with the proliferation of possibilities for human lives, the early egalitarianism was compromised. For at least the past seven millennia, the ethical lives of many societies have been torn between answering to the perspectives of all their members and maintaining the conditions that allow a rich menu of human possibilities (typically available only to a small elite). Progress can only be determined in the wake of a decision about the relative priority of the conflicting functions. *A complete concept of ethical progress presupposes a normative stance.*

Postpone, for the moment, any articulation and defense of a normative stance, and assume that the original function of ethics is not to be neglected. Specifically, suppose the elements of ethical practice that guard against potentially pervasive failures of responsiveness are to be prized, even if there are costs for fulfilling rival, conflicting functions. On that basis, we can pick out some progressive transitions in the history of ethical practice. For example, whenever societies began to insist that their members not tell one another things the informants believed to be false, they attempted to forestall a possibly enormous class of episodes in which speakers failed to respond to the recognizable wishes of their audiences. Ethical progress was made through accepting the precept that deception is wrong. Because human dependence on others for information and guidance would appear to be a permanent feature of our condition, as we envisage the further development of ethical practice we can only suppose that, so long as our descendants commit themselves to the original function of ethics, seeking to maintain those elements of practice that protect against widespread failures of responsiveness, they will preserve the prohibition of dishonesty. The precept will continue as a stable part of ethical practice, however we continue to make ethical progress. Taking a cue from the pragmatists, we can think of truth as what emerges in the indefinite march of progress—"Truth happens to an idea," as James says—thus inverting the idea of progress as the discovery of prior truth.

Secularists can thus rehabilitate a notion of ethical truth. They can defend a set of core ethical truths, rough generalizations corresponding to the good advice learned at parental knees. "Lying is wrong" is "true for the most part," or (in a more modern idiom) is a good default policy, undermined only when answering truthfully would exemplify an even greater failure of responsiveness: for responsiveness to others can occasionally be expressed in concealing the truth—when the audience intends to use the information to cause great harm, or when the questioner's deepest purposes would be subverted by a candid response.

So there is a touchstone for assessing the practices of different societies, something allegedly unavailable once the thought of an external standard, anchored in the transcendent, is forsworn. Yet if the normative stance used to elaborate the notion of ethical progress allows for different ways of compromising ethical functions to count as progressive, some ethical issues may be permanently irresoluble. Rival traditions that strike the compromise in different equally allowable ways may progress indefinitely without ever completely converging. Each may regard the other as committed to an attractive, if subordinate, ideal, an ideal it would be desirable to realize subject to fulfilling a function taken to be dominant. Societies emphasizing the importance of a rich set of options for human lives may try to achieve as much responsiveness to all their members as is possible without diminishing the menu of opportunities beyond a particular threshold; those committed to the egalitarian representation of all voices may attempt to proliferate the human possibilities, so long as they do not retreat too far from conditions of full equality. Drawn to the ideal they perceive in the alternative tradition, both groups may progress indefinitely, yet there may be no stage at which they reach a stable state exemplifying a unique right balance between the competing ideals. Some ethical questions—that of how exactly to trade conditions of equality against richness of possibilities for living, for example—may lack determinate answers.

IV

Does an account of this sort really meet the challenge directed against secular humanism? It is time to respond to some concerns and objections.

A first, obvious, worry is that viewing ethics as an outgrowth of social technology is incapable of accounting for ethical objectivity, for the simple reason that technologies inevitably depend on subjective preferences. Technologies are directed toward goals particular human beings want to achieve: people seek new forms of transportation, for example, because they would like to reach currently inaccessible places, or to go more easily or more speedily to destinations already within reach. Talk of problems suggests, misleadingly, that they are objective conditions, spurs to action quite independent of the agents' wants. That, suggests the critic, is a mistake: to be a problem is to be *felt* as a problem.

Although this line of objection embodies a genuine insight, it goes astray in making the concept of a problem entirely subjective— as can be seen immediately by recalling that people can have problems of which they are entirely unaware. The problems inspiring technological ventures are, to be sure, often identified, but they can be more or less objective insofar as they depend on desires that would arise with more or less frequency in a particular situation. In the extreme case, when *any* person placed in particular circumstances would develop a particular wish for change, it is wrong to dismiss the envisaged goal as "subjective." It is no idiosyncratic whim, but a natural outgrowth of the situation, testifying to the objectively problematic character of the circumstances. Medical examples bring out more clearly the objective face of problems. To say of someone with a broken leg, of someone suffering debilitating depression, or of someone in a crisis from cystic fibrosis that their problems are purely subjective, because they depend on particular desires—the wish to walk, to experience some vestiges of pleasure, to breathe—is as absurd as it is insensitive. The ethical case is similar. Limited responsiveness once pervaded all phases and all aspects of the lives of our human and hominid ancestors. We should endorse Dewey's wise judgment: "Moral conceptions and processes grow naturally out of the very conditions of human life."

The ethical project is inescapable. We who come late in it live in ways shaped by its achievements and its failures, but we have no option except to continue it, in some fashion or other. Equipped with a wider range of emotions and desires, able to envisage many possibilities for human existence and to ponder their worth, the only alternative to the ethical life we have is the condition shared by chimpanzees, bonobos, and our pre-ethical ancestors, a predicament surely even more abhorrent to us than it was to the pioneers who took the first steps in escaping from it. The record of human cruelty and indifference, even under the aegis of attempts to promulgate patterns for our conduct, undermines any optimistic thought that a few thousand generations of our species have equipped us with some greatly improved capacity for responsiveness. In a world where actions can easily have a profound impact on the lives of many invisible others, in which we are knitted together in a vast web of causal interactions, our lack of responsiveness has an enormously expanded field on which to play, and the old disease—the limited ability of human beings to perceive and to accommodate one another—can effloresce in extravagant symptoms, social tension, and conflict on a global scale.

Is that an argument for the normative stance I bluntly adopted earlier, for the assumption of the continued priority of the original function of ethics? Or is it intended as such? No, and no. The genealogy of the ethical project might teach us to be wary of the claims and arguments of individuals, and even of the hegemony of argument. For the thought of specific people as entitled to speak the last word on ethical matters was a consequential modification of a previously democratic project, a spinoff from an effective strategy for encouraging compliance to the precepts of the code, even when none of your fellows is able to monitor you. Conceiving ethics as the province of individual authoritative experts began in supposing a transcendent standard to which the authorities had special access. Among secular thinkers, it has survived in thinking of a ground of values that can be recognized and characterized by processes of individual reflection and reason, available in principle to all but perhaps in practice restricted to an especially wise or astute elite: the philosopher replaces the shaman and the priest.

The genealogy offers a different model of ethical decision and revision, one in which members of a group attempt to understand the perspectives of the others, and share a commitment to finding a resolution with which all can be satisfied. Nothing outside the human world directs the correct answer, but each human perspective is an essential part of the negotiation. To adopt this model would be to see the history of the ethical project as marked by fundamental distortions, as those who pretend to an authority they do not have leave long-lasting marks on ethical practice by inscribing their own predilections and prejudices in enduring precepts, in whose name vast numbers of human beings have been deemed suitable for domination or punishment. There is, however, a more modest form of expertise. Because people differ in their talents for formulating alternatives clearly, for suggesting considerations pro and con, and for highlighting questions it is useful to discuss, conversation and negotiation may reach conclusions satisfactory to all, or may reach them more easily, if individuals with particular qualities—perhaps those now hailed as religious teachers or as secular moralists—play the role of facilitating discussion. The revolutionary contributions of individual figures, many of them religious teachers, lie exactly here: John Woolman and Mary Wollstonecraft, Jesus and the Buddha, sparked important reflections and discussions (with which we are surely not yet finished). Even if philosophers cannot deliver authoritative solutions, philosophical midwifery may thrive—as the example of Socrates shows. Hence the attempt to settle matters by definitive demonstration gives way to proposals: try thinking of things this way.

Reasoning and argument have a place in the formulation of a normative stance, as they presumably did in the discussions of the small groups who decided on patterns for living together, but reasoning must be framed by a prior perspective about goals and procedures. I propose a framework, motivated by reflection on the history of the ethical project and by the hope that understanding what we have been up to will make progressive change more frequent and more systematic. Genealogical reflection invites the thought that ethical practice has been distorted by supposing an external standard and by crediting some individuals with special access to that standard. Because the objective problem of our limited responsiveness to others is pervasive and permanent, it should be at the center of *our* attention too, inspiring efforts to emulate the obvious strategy, achieved when our distant ancestors assembled all members of the group for discussions on terms of equality "in the cool hour." With respect to many issues arising for the continuation of the ethical project, the number of those potentially affected includes millions, even billions, among them some who are not yet born. Exact replication of the negotiations of our ancestors, or of contemporary hunter-gatherers, is impossible, but reflection on their procedures can suggest an ideal. Modification of ethical practice should flow from discussions among representatives of all points of view, each assigned equal status in the conversation, each freed from identifiable errors, and each dedicated to reaching conclusions all can accept.

Although no such ideal could be completely realized, steps to come closer to it are readily appreciated. *Actual* ethical discussions would be improved if there were representation of a broader diversity of perspectives, if the participants accepted a ban on appealing to substantive religious doctrines—for otherwise (given the arguments of the previous chapter) they would fall foul of the requirement to eradicate identifiable errors—and if they were predisposed, either by temperament or by training, to engage, at least in a detached setting, with the aspirations of others. Conversations of this sort are the best available vehicles for continuing the ethical project.

Conjoined with this methodological suggestion is a substantive proposal, one elaborating the idea of the continued centrality of the original problem of limited responsiveness. The earliest ethical negotiations almost certainly endorsed particular desires for all members of the group, desires for food, shelter, protection, and stability, for example. Focusing on that narrow repertoire of basic needs is inadequate for human beings to whom the ethical project has bequeathed a much more complex collection of emotions and aspirations. The fulfilling life is no longer delivered by supplying adequate food and regular sex, if indeed it ever was. The analogues of those originally endorsed desires are contemporary yearnings to have access to all the preconditions for a worthwhile life. Besides the basic resources required to continue existence from day to day, the preconditions include the provision of opportunities to appreciate a range of potential possibilities for human life and to choose freely among them (as Chapter 4 will propose in more detail). My secular ideal thus commits itself to making available to all people the human possibilities proliferated by the ethical project.

Earlier, the tension between maintaining equality and increasing the options for human existence was used to illustrate the phenomenon of functional conflict. Because that conflict runs so deep in the evolution of the ethical project, it must finally be addressed. Through demanding that all people be provided with the preconditions for choosing and pursuing lives of genuine worth, my proposal insists on a redistribution of the material resources collectively owned by our species, a redistribution sufficient to support the material and social bases whose current absence dooms many of the world's people to want and ill-health and ignorance and oppression and lack of choice. Among the primary ethical challenges of today is the task of reconfiguring the economic and political institutions that currently interfere with any such redistribution.

One worry about egalitarianism is that the economic arrangements it requires undermine the ability to maintain the resources it proposes to divide evenly: the pie shrinks and the equal shares become miserably small. Of course, the size of the shares depends not only on the dimensions of the pie but also on the number of diners. Egalitarians suppose it to be possible to find a set of economic arrangements, stably compatible with the form of redistribution envisaged, provided only that the human population is kept below a bound, a size taken to be, at worst, in the vicinity of the current total. (Whether this is overly optimistic is a matter for empirical inquiry.) A central element of my secularist proposal thus qualifies the traditional commandment to increase and multiply.

The loudest opposition to this proposed resolution of the functional conflict was voiced by Nietzsche, or by one of his personae. On the unlikely assumption that he would take my genealogy as an improvement on his own, Nietzsche would surely insist that, once the ethical project has brought forth a splendid array of human possibilities, its original function should have no hold on anyone—"free spirits" at any rate should devote themselves to developing and realizing the glorious forms of life of which they alone are capable. Yet this suggestion is made in a social vacuum. Supposing them to exist, the especially noble characters Nietzsche hails as "free spirits" do not emerge full-blown from the womb. Like the rest of us, they are nurtured and sustained by the social environments in which they mature. Whether any genetic markers would identify them in advance is highly dubious; that no currently known genetic markers do so is certain. Any attempt to realize Nietzsche's dreams for a world in which human possibilities are proliferated ever more richly by a small class of superior beings would be well advised to invest in all the possible candidates—and thus to ensure the preconditions of worthwhile lives for all. Ironically, the original function of ethics, in the form of the egalitarian ideal, retains its priority.

My sketch of a normative stance consists of two proposals, one focused on methods of ethical discussion, and the other a substantive egalitarian ideal to be entertained in such discussion. Together they fill out the concept of ethical progress, and so complete my secular account of values.

V

But why should anyone accept my proposals? What force do these claims about value have on anybody's conduct? The religious challenger and the philosopher who suspects ethical naturalism will join forces in raising such questions. I shall conclude this chapter with some brief answers.

Would-be naturalists are sometimes saddled with an impossible task. "Give us," says the critic, "some clearly defined mode of inference that leads from purely factual premises to the action-guiding normative conclusions you offer." But that is a bizarre demand. Human beings do not wander around the world, gathering facts and nothing but facts, until, one day, they launch themselves into ethical life by some specially adroit means of inference. From our earliest stages as thinking beings, we are immersed in a mixture of factual beliefs and value judgments, transmitted to us by our elders—we are "always already" ethical. Since the gradual unfolding of ethical life, tens of thousands of years ago, all our ancestors have been embedded in the ethical project. To repeat: ethical life is inescapable. The crucial question, one that might be formulated by asking for a specified mode of inference, is how to continue the project.

Part of the answer is easy. When functional harmony prevails—when it can be shown that a proposed modification of ethical practice better fulfills some functions and interferes with none—that suffices to justify the change. Functional conflict introduces complications. For instances of functional conflict, the critic can finally present his demand: "Specify a method of argument that will lead from factual statements—or, if you like, from the mix of factual beliefs and value-judgments embodied in current ethical practice—to a conclusion about the priority to be given to the conflicting functions!"

I have evaded the demand, retreating to weak talk of proposals and muttering about the hegemony of argument—or so at least it will seem to the critic. The proposals do not, however, descend from thin air. They are intended to be received against the background of a particular factual account, a narrative of what the ethical project has been and how it has evolved to yield the ethical life of the present. Although nobody knows how to specify a cogent method of inference leading from premises about the history of a practice to conclusions about how to continue that practice, I want to defend the reasonableness of accepting normative proposals by reflecting on the history of normative practices.

Reasonableness in belief is not always reducible to the generation of the pertinent beliefs according to formal rules or precise algorithms—the tendency of recent decades to substitute a narrow conception of rationality for the older, and looser, notion of what is reasonable notwithstanding. Examples from ethical life reveal changes of attitude in which people come to see themselves and their conduct differently. Many of us have had the humbling experience of learning that words and gestures produced with benign intent have been perceived quite differently by others; we have learned from those we have unwittingly hurt that what was said has caused pain and humiliation; we have come to see our ways of speaking—and thinking—as connected to sources of social domination. Episodes of this sort *reasonably* induce us to reconsider, to adopt a new perspective on what we characteristically say and do, to jettison old categories, to uproot old habits and to subscribe to new precepts. What occurs is not so much a different selection of statements from the same language as a shift of frame.

Or consider a related example with significantly different features. Some Victorian readers of *Bleak House* revised their attitudes toward the justice of the then current treatment of the urban poor. Appreciating the fact that Dickens had written a novel, not a sociological treatise, they did not read him as presenting new facts—they already knew, at least theoretically and probably empirically, that life in parts of London was brutal and squalid—they were moved to *feel* the awfulness of living in places like Tom-All-Alone's. Their feelings permeated their hearing of the novel's voices, voices praising the institutions provided for the destitute. Echoing the readers' own previous declarations, the voices resonated in their consciousness. Unable now to hear them as anything other than hollow, they could no longer pronounce their old judgments with any conviction. Dickens persuaded them—reasonably persuaded them—to feel larger sympathies for social reform.

Not only fact, but even fiction, can do philosophical, ethical, work. Argument must begin somewhere, and chains of inference depend not only on the premises but on the categories used in formulating them. None of us ever achieves a Cartesian point from which all principles can be scrutinized, all categories probed. Instead, we acquire a frame for our reasoning, picking it up relatively automatically from the contingent culture in which we grow. If we are to amend it or to improve it that must be as a result of being led to see matters differently. Facts about how others see our treatment of them, facts about the historical evolution of practices we acquire from a long tradition, even works of fiction and drama are the tools we have for achieving a change of perspective. Despite the tendency to underrate them, a few philosophers have recognized the worth of such tools: as Dewey remarks, "the arts, those of converse and the literary arts which are the enhanced continuations of social converse, have been the means by which goods are brought home to human perception."

Proposals of a normative stance are entirely reasonable if they are moved by thorough reflection on the historical evolution of the ethical project, and proposers are justified in attempts to enable others to share their vision. Nor should it be assumed that their reflections are second-rate substitutes for the superior methods of changing view available in more rigorous areas of inquiry. Major transitions in the history of the natural sciences, the episodes known (since Kuhn's seminal discussion) as "scientific revolutions," involve the same stocktaking, in which reflection on a body of partial successes and stubborn difficulties prompts new conceptions of which questions are most significant and what the standards for their resolution should be. In science as in ethics, judgment irreducible to any precise algorithms we can presently specify is sometimes unavoidable.

Treating values as products of negotiation, in which participants are sometimes moved by reflections on the history of ethical practice, may well seem to rob them of their dignity, and consequently of their force. Why should anyone feel bound to respect values so generated? The reply that they emerge from a project that has been constitutive of humanity, that has made us what we are, might elicit a shrug. Secular thinkers in other traditions, including some who draw inspiration from Kant, typically feel they can do better. We should respect the moral law, because failure to do so is to lapse from fundamental rational principles. Yet that, too, is powerless to prevent the shrug: Who should care about forfeiting what Kantians—tendentiously— call practical rationality? The source of Kant's well-merited influence lies in powerful images of the idealized agent: as the exemplification of reason, as an intrinsic source of value, as a legislator among equals. Behind the misleading advertisements for "*a priori* foundations" stand ventures in reasonable persuasion, of the same general type as those figuring in my articulation of secular humanism. Because the latter attends more closely to our ethical practices and their history, it should, I suggest, be seen as the basis of conceptions more apt for guiding the continuation of the ethical project.

As these remarks suggest, there is an important kinship between the approach I have advocated and a Kantian form of humanism. Secular Kantians often view moral principles—and objectively valid value judgments more generally—as generated by special forms of reasoning whose character is determined independently of contingent human preferences and emotions (and is therefore, in an important sense, "external"). On one interpretation of his ideas, Kant displaced the source of ethical objectivity from the transcendent to the realm of reason, a kingdom (or republic?) supposedly governed by *a priori* laws. I propose a further transformation. Instead of abstracting from our actual characteristics and our actual history, I take the grounds of value to lie in the reasonings and conversations in which we engage with one another, as we struggle to cope with fundamental features of the human predicament, in particular with our existence as social beings whose capacity to respond to others is limited. So, in addressing skeptical questions, where some Kantians are inclined to flourish their allegedly *a priori* principles of practical reason to confute the skeptic as falling into contradiction, I diagnose an attempt to abandon an inescapable human project. To the extent that the Kantian response succeeds, so does mine.

At last the original challenge can be addressed. According to the challenger, a religious grounding of values delivers a status no secular alternative can mimic. How exactly? If the suggestion is that values derive from the divine will, it must address the questions Socrates posed to Euthyphro—as well, of course, as defending the existence of the favored deity (or deities) against the arguments of the previous chapter. Retreating to a less definite position, in which the transcendent is identified with the pattern for our conduct, seen as "the ethical order of the cosmos," raises obvious concerns about how we can be guided by a source supposed to be inaccessible to us. Anyone who worries why she should care about the values generated by continuing the ethical project should be equally concerned about obeying an "ethical order" so dimly characterized. In the end, religious foundations provide no better answer to skepticism than do the humanistic approaches, whether Kantian or my preferred alternative. Whatever is said cannot ward off the (Faustian?) shrug.

For all that I have said, when ethics is detached from religion, a sense of loss may linger. When the great religious revolutionaries—Jesus and the Buddha, for example—are recast as initiators of a thoroughly secular conversation, directed at problem solving, ethical life may seem reduced, a wan substitute for something far richer. Chapter 5 will return to this issue as part of a general concern about the shallowness of secular existence. For the moment, however, it may be useful to recall that the focal problems for ethics include one, namely the problem of limited responsiveness, that is central to our lives, and that the problem is addressed in all surviving ethical traditions by connecting ethical prescriptions to a broad range of human emotions, almost all of which are independent of religious belief. Those who feel pride in upholding principles enjoining aid, who take joy in cooperation with others, who are deeply imbued with a sense of solidarity, who feel gratitude, respect, and even awe in contemplating the deeds of the great exemplars of altruism are not detached technocrats, but people who can be inspired to discuss reforms of their ethical codes, even when the revolutionary proposals do not wear the robes of any religion.

My version of secularism places humanity at the center of value. It does not need a detour through some dim and remote transcendent. Nor does it see vivid vindication of human worth in supposing, whether literally or metaphorically, that we are children or servants of God. My naturalism conceives us as both creators and loci of value, our work of creation prompted by the exigencies of the human predicament. Out of that work, carried forward in the ethical project, has come nothing less than a transformation of human existence, through the forging of connections among people and through the expansion of the possibilities of human lives. As we reflect on that transformation, we may regret some, even many, of the details, but we can only affirm—and celebrate—the project itself, constitutive as it is of who we have become. That, I suggest, is dignity of values enough.

THREE

RELIGION REFINED

I

The common reaction that the arguments of secular critics target only the crudest and least sophisticated forms of religion, leaving what the most thoughtful and sensitive believers cherish untouched, often provokes the critics to pose an exasperated question: "What exactly is this refined religion that escapes our objections?" My aim in this chapter is to say, as sympathetically and precisely as I can, what those who advocate a purer and more subtle form of religion have in mind. One of the hazards of any venture at clarifying this issue is, of course, that I shall exhibit another version of secularist incomprehension.

The case for doubt I launched in Chapter 1 depended on three assumptions: religions are conceived as bodies of doctrine; doctrinal statements are read by assuming everyday implications of the words used in formulating them; and faith in doctrine is not subordinated to ethical constraints. Refined religion abandons all three assumptions. First, religion is not understood as primarily a collection of doctrines about the transcendent, but as a system of practices and commitments. Second, the doctrinal statements that figure in religious practices and in expressions of commitment are not interpreted through the lens of everyday implications—they are taken to have symbolic significance, to be allegories or to contain profound metaphors. Third, the fundamental commitments of religions are to values, and the thought of a "transcendent realm" is important because of its role in articulating these commitments: perhaps the transcendent is identified with the source of values, or the acceptance of the transcendent is seen as spurring attempts to realize the values, or faith in the transcendent is taken to provide assurance that the values can be—or even will be—realized. Instead of going to the scriptures in search of new ethical truths, the refined believer identifies the ethical order independently, and espouses a religion because that religion expresses and promotes what is most deeply and enduringly valuable.

Brief explanations can only give the rough shape of the position. We need to go more slowly, and a useful place to start is with the symmetry argument of Chapter 1. A natural response to that argument would be to seek the "core doctrine" of the world's religions. Instead of trying to resolve the substantial conflicts (and thereby lapsing into dogmatism), the response would concede that all religions make many assertions that are (literally) false, but also affirm a shared truth. When the focus is on religions as bodies of doctrine, and when the language of doctrinal formulations is understood by importing everyday implications of the words employed, trying to evade the symmetry argument in this way is ineffective: the diversity of conceptions of the transcendent dooms the suggested "core doctrine" to vacuity. Gods and spirits, ancestors and mystic forces and sacred places lack any significant shared features—unless the "least common denominator" is presented in *normative* terms. The transcendent, which defies detailed human description, is worthy of special emotional attitudes, of reverence, of awe, of devotion.

So understood, the world's religions can be appreciated as invoking an aspect of reality—the transcendent—that exceeds any human ability to describe it in literal language. What, then, of the myriad conflicting doctrinal statements? These should be read, one and all, through and through, as metaphorical, allegorical, and poetic. In their diverse ways, religious traditions gesture toward the transcendent, supplying their adherents with figurative expressions to guide thought and conduct. Secular humanists are correct to recognize the symmetry among the processes through which doctrines are transmitted, sustained, and modified, and to be skeptical that such processes could reliably issue in the acceptance of true substantive doctrines. Strictly speaking, all doctrinal statements are false, for that is the way of figures of speech. In appraising the affirmations demanded of the devout in rival traditions, evidence and factual truth are not the issue. The crucial question concerns the capacity of metaphors, myths, and stories to orient the lives of the faithful in valuable ways: pose William James's insistent demand, and ask if the "fruits for life" are good. As we shall see, raising that question across the spectrum of the world's religions and through the course of their historical development might elicit judgments about the progress or backsliding of particular religions, as well as assessments of some traditions as superior to others. Nonetheless, even if complete symmetry prevailed, that would be no tragedy, but would simply register an odd quirk of history, the ability of all human cultures to generate equally effective metaphors for coping with a significant, but indescribable aspect of reality.

Soft atheism acknowledges the bare possibility of the transcendent, but regards the present assertion of any such aspect of reality as entirely unwarranted. Refined religion need not quarrel with that assessment. Accepting the transcendent, and particular stories and images as gestures toward it, may be based on faith. As Clifford saw, leaping beyond the evidence is often ethically suspect—but it would plainly be permissible if the product of faith were a commitment to the ethical itself. The most straightforward version of refined religion identifies the transcendent as the source of values and virtues, ideals and duties. In some of his (highly varied and apparently incompatible) characterizations of religion, James makes that identification. To be a religious person is to affirm what is valuable, to say "Yes" to "the eternal things"—where these include not only moral principles but also the deepest ideals and values. At the core of religion, then, is not a body of doctrine, a collection of descriptions of the transcendent, but a commitment to values that are external to (independent of) the believer, and indeed to all human beings. Doctrine only enters in the guise of metaphors and stories, apt for conveying the most fundamental values and for guiding the devout toward realizing them.

II

Refined religion escapes the secularist argument by diverging from the assumptions on which that argument depends. An obvious worry is that success is achieved only through so attenuating the notion of religion that the resultant perspective is no longer worthy of the name. At the heart of the religious attitude is faith, understood as commitment to an objective order of values, a commitment shared among many religious traditions (although perhaps not by those that have failed to take crucial progressive steps). The world's religions articulate faith as a commitment to particular values, perhaps all of them shared (at least among the major traditions), and subsequently to a specific ordering of values, about which there can be divergence and conflict among rival traditions. None of this, however, distinguishes refined religion from secular perspectives that maintain the existence of objective values, and take the world's cultures as advancing conceptions of an independent ethical order, with some universal features and some areas of disagreement. Has religion been "refined" only by collapsing it into realism about values?

Refined religion can differentiate itself from secular endorsement of an independent ethical order in three distinct ways. First, and most obviously, it adopts the picture of a two-tier universe. Beyond the physical, organic, human realm there is a higher level, with a special connection to values: on the "straightforward" version of refined religion, sketched in the previous section, the transcendent just is the ground of values. The worth of human lives and the moral status of human deeds are measured not by any relations that prevail within the physical, organic, human domain, the lower level, but through their relation to the transcendent, the higher tier. In this spirit, Kierkegaard's claims about the "suspension of the ethical" can be reinterpreted, less literally and more sympathetically, by envisaging the possibility that the mundane ethics of human relations is superseded and deepened by a higher order of ethical life, grounded in the transcendent. Many religious believers are drawn to a picture of this kind, and it is one source of the frequent challenge that secularists are unable to offer any adequate account of values (the challenge Chapter 2 attempted to turn back). Ironically, as the next section will argue, even when it is refined, religion faces greater difficulties on this score.

A second, evident difference between the refined believer and the secular adherent of an objective order of values is emphasized by sociological accounts of religion, from Durkheim on. Commitment to the transcendent is embedded within an array of practices— ceremonies, rites, and community projects—which are the primary elements of the religious life. Buddhism, Hinduism, Judaism, Christianity, and Islam can all be developed so as to abandon the literal truth of tales about the transcendent, while retaining the rituals, community structures, shared ethical endeavors, and even the credal avowals of their more literalist relations. Sometimes, those for whom doctrinal statements are metaphorical through and through may mingle peacefully with their cousins whose declarations make more substantive claims about the transcendent. Other people, inspired by elements of different religions, may integrate parts of disparate traditions in a novel eclectic synthesis. Yet others, like Emerson, may start explicitly from an abstract notion of the transcendent, and consider the design of substitutes for the rites and community structures of neighboring religious life. Distinctive parts of antecedent religious practice are thus preserved, modified, recombined, or refashioned, always subject to the basic requirement that, when doctrinal statements are pondered or uttered, they are interpreted figuratively. As in the case of the two-tier universe, this way of separating refined religion from secular realism about values comes with a challenge for the secularist: The practices at the core of religious life are essential if people are to cope with their mortality and with the potential meaninglessness of their lives (a challenge the next chapter will take up).

The third (and last) way of differentiating refined religion from secular commitments to an independent order of values follows James in supposing particular types of emotion to pervade the attitude to the transcendent. Acceptance of a higher realm that is the source of values is accompanied by solemnity and awe, by a humble willingness to subordinate and redirect the impulses of the self, and yet a joyful acquiescence in the discipline. What stoics must labor to accept is welcomed gladly. The religious life unfolds with confidence and hope, seeing the existence of the higher tier of reality as a promise that values can be sought and at least partially achieved. Here, too, emerges a challenge for secular humanists: When human lives are bereft of these important emotions toward the transcendent, they are diminished, perhaps through the loss of dimensions of experience available to the believer, perhaps through the inadequacy of any purely secular discipline to govern the darker impulses intrinsic to human nature (Chapter 5 will take up this challenge).

Refined religion is a genuine alternative to secular perspectives, and it poses questions secular humanism must answer. We should also consider, however, how well refined religion does with those very questions.

III

Chapter 2 juxtaposed a naturalistic attempt to vindicate values with a simple account of the transcendent ground of ethical principles. Certain actions or ways of living are right or wrong, good or bad, valuable or worthless because of the deity's (or deities') attitudes toward them. Refined religion must disavow this simple story. On the one hand, introducing a divine commander would violate the concession that all substantive doctrines about the transcendent are false; on the other, it would confront the dilemma Socrates posed to Euthyphro. The straightforward version of refined religion solves both problems at a stroke. Canceling the separation between a transcendent person and what is valuable, it identifies the transcendent with value itself (the transcendent just *is* the Valuable, the Good, and so forth). No deity is invoked, nor does Socrates have the opportunity to pose his question.

Yet this escape comes at a price. It is assumed that religious believers are at least partially successful in apprehending what is genuinely valuable. If that were not so, there would be no reason to take their faith as focusing on the real source of values. Clifford's doubts would return with full force. People who simply guessed that certain goals are valuable or that particular types of action are ethically permitted, and who then acted on their speculations, would be as ethically problematic as their counterparts who leap to factual conjectures beyond the evidence. To judge that a religious tradition furnishes images, metaphors, parables, and myths that help make comprehensible and vivid important ideals presupposes the capacity for discerning what those ideals are. How does the refined believer do it?

One potential answer would propose that the truth about value is revealed through the authoritative declarations of a particular religious tradition (or perhaps through declarations occurring in all major religious traditions). Unfortunately, the proposal threatens a regression to a conception refined religion is supposed to have abandoned, that of a knowable transcendent. Moreover, it pitches the refined believer into an awkward predicament. Unless the believer can *herself* recognize what is valuable, she lacks any basis for counting the tradition(s) as authoritative. Authority cannot be judged by focusing on ancillary characteristics—even though commandments are promulgated by people with great power, though scriptural texts have exceptional grandeur and beauty, that would not justify a believer in following them. Many historical atrocities have been carried out by people who followed the dictates of powerful and eloquent leaders. Assessing ethical authority rests on a prior capacity for identifying what is valuable. As Kant already saw, recognizing the "Holy One of Israel" as perfect is possible only for people who have an independent ability to judge the good.

Refined religion has two possible strategies for escaping this predicament. One, popular with intellectually well articulated religions—Eastern as well as Western—seeks support from secular philosophy. Since (at least) Augustine, Christian thinkers have borrowed metaphysical and epistemological ideas to elaborate their conceptions of value. Not only Plato—Augustine's favorite source—but Aristotle, Kant, and the post-Kantian Idealists have left their imprint on versions of Christian doctrine, as well as on Judaism and Islam. Sometimes, the metaphysics and epistemology co-opted fit well with the two-tier picture of the universe: Plato's commitment to the Form of the Good, to which particularly talented and well-educated people ultimately have access, is the most obvious example. On other occasions the borrowing disrupts attempts to preserve the *religious* features in refined religion. To follow Kant in identifying the requirements of pure practical reason as the source of what is morally right would leave the refined believer with a spartan concept of the "transcendent" as the "realm of reason." Whether, so construed, the "transcendent" is worthy of the name, the identification threatens to eviscerate the attractive picture of the two-tier universe, to undermine the idea of specifically religious emotions, and to hollow out religious rites and practices. All three barriers erected in the previous section to mark off refined religion from a purely secular position are in danger of collapse.

Envisaging a two-tier universe, in which the superior—transcendent—tier is characterizable only in figurative language, and in which the ethical values governing human interactions and achieved in human relationships are seen as derivative from transcendent sources of value, places obvious strain on the task of providing any convincing explanation of how faith comes to be focused on what is *genuinely* valuable. Even worse, the erection of an allegedly higher level of values interferes with a thorough appreciation of human beings as sources of value and obstructs a clear vision of our relatedness to one another. However generously you read Kierkegaard's celebration of Abraham, it is hard to quell the concern that the "subsidiary characters," Isaac and Rebecca, vanish from the story and from the analysis: their claims go unheard. By treating human ethical life as a peculiar projection from an allegedly higher realm, human beings and their problems become subordinated to something supposedly vaster and greater. Secular humanism admits the bare possibility of the transcendent, but, until it shows up in our lives, thinks we do better to collapse the two-tier universe and to focus firmly and clearly on the human.

Chapter 2 argued for a naturalistic approach to values, partly inspired by suspicion of extant secular accounts of the metaphysics and epistemology of value. Even if its conclusions are too strong, however, the most plausible rival approaches to value—liberalized versions of Kantianism or other types of constructivism—are the least hospitable to the straightforward version of refined religion that takes the transcendent as the source of value. Would-be alliances with philosophy offer only a problematic strategy. Better for refined religion to take a more radical step.

The transcendent may play a role in ethical life without serving as the source of value. Refined religion may contend that values are identified by means of some thoroughly secular processes—perhaps even the routes envisaged in the previous chapter—and insist on the propriety of a leap of faith that views these values as in harmony with something transcendent. To take the leap is to provide human subjects with a keener sense of the importance of the values and to endow them with hope, even with confidence, that the most worthy ideals can be realized. In this mode, refined religion allows the principles for ethical life to be articulated through secular forms of investigation. Faith adds a depth and seriousness to that life. The pallid picture of social technology is transformed into the passionate embrace of moral commitments: ethical life becomes more "strenuous."

Chapter 5 will consider this suggestion more carefully. For the moment, however, I want to link this more cautious version of refined religion to one of the masterpieces of religious literature, Paul's poem in the thirteenth chapter of his first letter to the Corinthians. If, as I have argued, the problem of limited responsiveness lies at the core of the ethical project, the ideal of extending love to all, even if practically unattainable, furnishes an inspiring direction for our attitudes and actions. For people who accept that ideal and celebrate the priority of the gospels' second commandment, faith in a connection to something vaster, to a transcendent, might not only intensify ethical commitment but also fill them with hope that loving relations can be ever more extensively realized. Thus, as Paul suggests, faith, hope, and love are bound together. But one value is dominant—"the greatest of these is love."

To sum up, refined religion, in its most straightforward version, identifies the transcendent as the source of values, and thereby faces the difficulty of explaining how the genuine values are identified. Until an account has been supplied, there is a major lacuna in the position. Hence I have envisaged a possible retreat, in which faith in the transcendent serves to deepen and motivate ethical commitments whose grounding lies elsewhere.

IV

The worries of the previous section are not the most common secular concerns about forms of religion that attempt to evade the commitments of literalism. More usually, the charge is that "sophisticated" forms of religion replace a picture clear enough to be judged—and to be recognized as false—with something too nebulous to be assessed, or even understood. Perhaps the clouds make it impossible to identify the issue discussed in the previous section, to see how taking the transcendent to be the source of values raises a serious issue about how those values are identified.

Refined religion has a long career, extending deep into the history of the five major world religions. In the post-Enlightenment West, it is formulated self-consciously in response to secular critique. During the past century or so, versions of it have been defended by religious sympathizers, from William James and Martin Buber to Paul Tillich and Robert Bellah. Plainly, all its champions want to distance the religion they respect—and often adopt—from claims that particular statements apparently about events in the natural world, involving Abraham or Jesus or Muhammad, are literally true. But then mysterious locutions begin to appear in their expositions. There is talk of "higher truth," of "different orders of reality," and the like. Impatient secularists despair of making sense of these idioms, and, suspecting the stratagem of sanctuary in indefiniteness, they view "sophistication" as a cover for sophistry.

In my view, not only is this reaction uncharitable but it also truncates a potentially fruitful discussion. The task of the next sections will be to elaborate a framework in which the claims of refined religion can be presented more definitely and with greater precision. Achieving that framework helps secular humanism as well. For a focused view of refined religion makes its differences with secular humanism more vivid, thereby sharpening the questions secularists should address.

As we have seen, refined religion sidesteps the symmetry argument by taking an ecumenical approach to the world's religions. Yet its proponents do not want to rest with the bare claim that belief in a transcendent reality is permissible. They hope to defend a "religious pluralism," in which the "stories" of the major religious traditions (and possibly of all religions) are conceived as valuable responses to different human situations. Of course, they are not literally true, and therefore can be classified as myths. But—and here secularists become uneasy—they are "true myths." Despite the conflicts among them, each is "worthy of belief," and, indeed, a sophisticated religious mind can embrace all of them.

The appearance of mystery-mongering is compounded by tendencies to talk about reality in unrestrained ways. Allegedly, we live in a number of "different worlds." Although our "paramount reality" is "the world of daily life"—a world for which everyday factual language provides an accurate, but partial, description, one deepened and extended by the languages of the rigorous sciences—we can escape to "other realities." In dreams, in play, in sports, in reading or in watching films, we visit "other worlds," and the visits are important to us, satisfying needs that contact with the "paramount reality" cannot address. The world's religions construct even more significant "realities." Entering them, people discover fulfillment for their deepest yearnings. Deprived of them, human existence would be empty or shallow or debased.

My brief summary accentuates the features that provoke secular impatience. "True myth" invites the riposte that it is an oxymoron. Thoughts of embracing "conflicting myths" or touring among "multiple realities" portray subtle religious thinkers as trying to follow the advice the White Queen gave Alice—to believe six impossible things before breakfast. Critics imbued with a sense that all this is mere muddle will conclude that attempts to refine religion provide no alternative to forthright secularism.

At the heart of the puzzling formulations are two difficult concepts: *truth* and *world*. I shall argue that references to "different worlds" introduce tangles refined religion would do better to avoid. Nevertheless, an exploration of the varieties of truth exposes a clear, and interesting, set of themes refined believers are attempting to sound.

V

Philosophers like to talk about "the world," and other writers, waxing philosophical, follow suit. Typically, however, the ambiguity of 'world' escapes notice. Sometimes, the world is conceived as that to which we respond in our experience, that we affect by our actions, and, most fundamentally, that in which we are placed. From this perspective, "the world" is correlative with "the self"—however the self is identified, the world is the container in which it sits, everything that stands apart from it. So far, there is only a minimal structure, a privileged object—the self—and everything else.

Often, however, we operate with a richer conception of the world, one in which it is constituted in space and time, contains a wide variety of objects, is divided into kinds of things, is full of causal relations and natural processes. This world is richly structured. Moreover, a structured world is partially culturally constituted. What counts as a single object depends on human decision—boundaries (in time as well as in space) have to be *drawn*. How the objects cluster into kinds also rests on our determinations: what counts as family or bird or motion has been differently fixed at different historical stages and in different cultures. Worlds in this richer sense change when people revise their ideas about the boundaries of objects or about how to classify things together or even when they reconceive the normal course of a process. Galileo changed the world when he taught us to see swinging stones as pendulums. Yet, in a sparer sense, the world remains the same: the containing stuff (relatively unstruc-tured) is as it always was.

Appreciating the two senses of "world" is a major insight of prag-matism, from James and Dewey to their contemporary successors. The fruitful pragmatist theme is that the worlds in which we live— the worlds-of-objects-divided-into-kinds-with-standards-of-normal-functioning-etc.—are structured in part by us, in ways that depend both on our psychological faculties and on our purposes. These richer worlds are important to us, for it is only about them that we can ask (for example) how many things they contain, or how their constituents relate in space and time, let alone pose all our less abstract, more mundane questions. Creatures with different senses live in different worlds—the world of the bat is not the human world. People, whose psychological apparatus is constant but whose ends evolve, also come to inhabit different worlds.

Among human purposes are those of commonsense inquiry and of the various sciences. Although it is often suggested that science (singular) aims at an all-encompassing account of nature, dreams of a complete final theory are fantasies—probably unattainable in prin-ciple, and almost certainly unrealizable in practice. Instead, our everyday investigations and their counterparts in the developed sci-ences try to find out about bits and pieces of the world (in the bare, relatively unstructured sense). They try to organize it in thought, and sometimes in physical rearrangement, so that particular parts are or-dered, subject to intervention and prediction and understanding. These are important human purposes, but they are by no means the only ones. Some parts of our world-construction draw boundaries around objects, group them into kinds, and set standards for normal processes so as to facilitate the work of controlling our environment, but we also devise ways of thinking and of organizing experience to pursue different goals. As the champions of refined religion suggest, we do this in play, in literature and in art, in our ethical life—and in religion.

Yet the language of "world construction" and of "multiple realities" among which we move is tricky, and it is easy to ignore the limits of human powers to "remake" the world. There are two kinds of constraints on restructuring the world, one stemming from us (our faculties, our purposes) and the other from what the world—in the bare, relatively unstructured sense—will let us do in remaking it. Galileo changed the world by giving old objects a new Gestalt: swinging stones became (imperfect) pendulums. But he was not able to work magic, introducing new objects, perfect pendulums, for there have been none of those, either before his time or since. Refined religion raises secular hackles when it seems to extend the reach of world-construction, invoking "realities" in ways that flout a crucial constraint.

To appreciate how the pragmatist insight can be misapplied, and thus to deploy it cautiously, it is useful to turn from 'world' to 'truth.' Jesting Pilate asked "What is truth?" Philosophers who take the question seriously often defend a single answer. Refined religion, however, must suppose that there are several species of truth. For it concedes that, taken specifically, all the doctrinal statements of the world's religions are false, and yet that these statements belong to "true myths." On the one hand, there is something that might be called "factual truth" or "scientific truth" or "descriptive truth" (the species of truth that has figured throughout my previous discussions), and by its lights the statements of myths are not true; on the other hand, there is a different mode of truth, one that must ultimately be explained. As we shall see shortly, refined religion can lapse into confusion if it treats "mythical truth" as if it were factual truth, invoking an "alternative reality" to answer to correct mythical description.

From Aristotle on, a popular account of factual truth has deployed the idea of a correspondence between symbols and reality, an idea finally articulated in the twentieth century with logical precision. Consider a simple sentence from the New Testament, "Jesus wept." Plausibly, this counts as factually true—for the name 'Jesus' in English refers to a historical person who once exemplified the property of shedding tears (the property picked out by the English verb 'wept'). By contrast, sentences such as "Jesus rose from the dead" or "Moses talked with God" or "Muhammad heard the word of Allah" do not count as factually true. For, even if we suppose that all three names ('Jesus,' 'Moses,' 'Muhammad') pick out definite historical figures, those people did not have the properties the sentences ascribe to them. To contend that these sentences are true—constituents of true myths—a different notion of truth must be invoked.

So far, a correspondence between words and things (and between words and properties) has given us a conception of truth for sentences in a particular language (English). Yet when we are thinking of truth as *what we aim at in our inquiries*, the simple idea of truth-in-a-language is too weak. With respect to many human purposes, including those of central concern to refined religion, the important notion is truth (period). Full-blooded truth presupposes a pragmatic constraint: what we hail as factually true takes for granted the thought that the language of the formulation answers to the purposes of making the description. According to the gospel story, Pilate's question was prompted by Jesus' declaration that he bore witness to the truth. Neither of them should have been content with an answer that only specified truth-in-a-language. The idea of a pragmatic constraint on truth (period) will play an important role in understanding refined religion.

As already noted, refined religion needs an account of mythical truth that can apply to statements acknowledged as factually false. Talk of "multiple realities," rampant with opportunities for meta-physical confusion, is easily generated if mythical truth is assimilated to the model of factual truth. To see this, it helps to return to one of the practices sometimes viewed as taking us beyond the "world of daily life."

Arthur Conan Doyle wrote a series of novels and short stories about a character much beloved by his readers (albeit sometimes much resented by the author himself). These popular works are pieces of fiction, and most of the sentences they contain are not factually true. "Sherlock Holmes lived in Baker Street" is factually false, since 'Sherlock Holmes' picks out nothing in the world, and there is thus no pertinent candidate for possessing the property of having lived in Baker Street ('Baker Street' does refer to a part of the world, although 221B Baker Street has only recently come to exist—as a response to the popularity of the Sherlock Holmes stories). Yet it is tempting to say that the sentence is true, at least "in some sense." A rash way of developing the idea extends the correspondence approach to factual truth: apart from mundane reality, there is another "reality," the world of the stories, in which 'Sherlock Holmes' does pick out a person, and in which the person identified has the property of living in the place designated by 'Baker Street.' But what is this "other reality"? How do we engage with it when we read Conan Doyle's stories? How does it relate to the world (in the bare sense)?

Fortunately, there is a far better way to elaborate the idea that "in some sense" the sentence is true. Our world once contained an author, Conan Doyle, who produced a series of books. Those books *endorse* particular sentences in which the name 'Sherlock Holmes' occurs. Endorsement is sometimes explicit, when the sentence actually occurs in a story. On other occasions, endorsement is a matter of implication: even if we are never told explicitly that Sherlock Holmes had a navel, standard anatomy is something to be taken for granted. Yet endorsement is a complicated notion. Although the stories endorse the claim that Sherlock Holmes possessed a pipe, they do not endorse any specification of the number of pipes the detective owned.

Instead of taking fictional truth to be correspondence to some mysterious reality, we do better to conceive fictional truth as a matter of endorsement. Yet, just as the correspondence notion of truth-in-a-language has a stronger counterpart, the concept of factual truth (period), so too with fictional truth. People who declare that great works of literature deliver truth, as when the eminent late Victorian critic A. C. Bradley contends that "Shakespeare's fictions were truth," do not intend the banality that the fictions they admire contain sentences. They suppose that literature can answer to significant human purposes, and that some parts of some works play a profound role in fulfilling those ends. Once again, truth is subjected to a pragmatic constraint, indeed a demanding one—with respect to fictions and fictional truth, many are called but few are chosen.

Some of Conan Doyle's readers become so taken with his famous detective that they pursue, individually or collectively, all kinds of investigations into details of life in late Victorian London. Few of them are confused into thinking that Sherlock Holmes himself might figure among the objects of their discovery. They separate the "world of daily life" from the "world of the stories." Nevertheless, talk of the latter world might easily lapse into muddle if the boundaries were not clearly drawn. The two "worlds" overlap—if they did not, the activities of the Sherlockians would make no sense.

Nobody is likely to propose that Conan Doyle's stories are so attuned to our cultural needs, so apt, that they should prompt revision of the world of daily life, to include Sherlock Holmes among its denizens. Yet a similar temptation can easily arise with respect to myth. Assuming that mythical truth is grounded in a correspondence relation to some "other reality" eases a fall from refined religion to an unrefined counterpart. Treating fictional truth as centered on endorsement helps avoid both the temptation and the fall.

The ground is now prepared for understanding the limits of our world-making. Juxtaposing two scientific cases brings out the point. The pre-Copernican world was one in which the earth did not count among the planets; that world gave way in the seventeenth century to a world based on different principles of organization, in which the earth was grouped with Mars, Venus, and the other known planets, even seen as akin to bodies revolving around other suns. Here it is reasonable to talk of a change in the world of daily life (or, perhaps, in the daily life of the cognoscenti). Yet the reclassification left the population of heavenly bodies unchanged—in this respect it was quite unlike the later discoveries of Uranus, Neptune, and Pluto (or the recent debates about whether Pluto should be demoted).

In the chemical revolution of the late eighteenth century, processes of combustion were reclassified as episodes of absorption rather than of emission. The chemical community abandoned the thesis that combustible things share a common substance (or "principle"), phlogiston, given off in combustion. As in the Copernican case, the classification of items in the world changed. But we should not think that this world-change is more radical, that the newer chemical world discarded a substance belonging to its predecessor. Phlogiston *never* existed. World changes can draw the boundaries of objects in different places, group the same things in different ways, or see processes against the background of a different standard (as Galileo did with the pendulum), but their powers to populate the world with new beings are limited. Defined as "the substance emitted in combustion," the term 'phlogiston' always failed to pick out any part of reality, of the world (in the bare sense).

VI

Genuine insights about "religious truth" and "mythical truth" can easily be distorted by framing them in terms of "different worlds" or "multiple realities." Avoiding an inflated inventory of what there is proves easier if we think instead of different species of truth. A cursory look at fictional truth has illustrated the point. The next step is to undertake a more systematic investigation.

One of the seminal ideas of Wittgenstein's later philosophy is his insistence on the variety of uses of language. Not all of the things we do with words should be assimilated to the paradigm of describing or "stating the facts." Yet the diverse language-games we play have rules and criteria for playing them properly and successfully. Each game has a point, a goal the players try to achieve. The aims are various, but, for each game, the pertinent goal picks out a privileged class of statements, the ones the players intend to produce. Those are the *true* statements. From the diverse genus of aims arise the different species of truth.

Wittgenstein repeatedly warns his readers against assuming that the point is always to describe, and, in doing so, he protests the hegemony of factual truth (understood in terms of correspondence of symbols to things and properties). Assuming the permissibility of talking of "fictional truth," the discussion of the last section already illustrates the point—but hard-headed skeptics worry about so permissive a usage. Fortunately, we can turn to a domain in which talk of truth is well established. Following Wittgenstein's lead, the example of mathematics can be used to expose the metaphysical peculiarities resulting from failure to heed the warnings.

Supposing mathematical truth to be correspondence to reality requires acceptance of a vast realm of mathematical entities, needed to serve as the referents of the singular terms mathematicians use ('2,' 'the empty set,' and so on). Many philosophers (and some mathematicians) have acquiesced more or less regretfully in this Platonism, even though it brings in its train awkward questions about how we are able to refer to mathematical objects or to know anything about them. The mysteries, and the troubles they bring, can be avoided entirely by taking Wittgenstein's advice and thinking of mathematical truth in a different fashion.

Most mathematicians spend all their lives manipulating symbols within systems they have inherited from others: they play symbolic games whose rules are already laid down. Statements (or formulae) they produce count as true just in case they can be reached by the established rules. Yet there's a pragmatic condition on the games they play. The games must be worth playing. Some of the systems are very ancient, introduced millennia ago to cope with operations of regrouping objects and matching them, or of laying down units along a stretch of land. Out of the very basic games, those played in arithmetic and geometry, come other questions that call for extended notation and novel systems. The history of mathematics is punctuated by moments in which new symbolic games are introduced, perhaps to cope with physical, biological, or social phenomena, perhaps to answer questions raised by earlier games but unanswerable within them, perhaps to generalize earlier games, perhaps because the new games are aesthetically appealing or offer satisfying recreation. As new games are introduced, explored, and extended, unprecedented connections are sometimes forged between mathematical language and the parts of the world investigated by the natural and social sciences. The games mathematicians play acquire novel practical uses.

Looking at almost any historical episode in which mathematicians have significantly extended the language they use will expose the advantages of my preferred approach. Hamilton's introduction of quaternions offers a compelling instance. Inspired by his recognition that the arithmetic and algebra of complex numbers could be developed systematically by treating complex numbers as ordered pairs of real numbers and specifying laws for the addition and multiplication of the pairs, Hamilton sought a three-dimensional analogue. Quickly becoming convinced that no such generalization would succeed, he focused on the four-dimensional case, endeavoring to work out the addition and multiplication tables for quadruples of real numbers— "quaternions" as he called them. Addition proved no problem, but the search for an acceptable multiplication table took years. Finally, by abandoning the commutativity of multiplication, Hamilton found a scheme that would satisfy his other constraints—and carved the crucial equation into the stonework of a Dublin bridge.

We have some information about what happened in the intervening years of frustration. Hamilton would enter his study in the morning, and emerge much later—greeted by his wife with the plaintive question "Have you discovered quaternions yet?"—having covered sheet after sheet of paper with explorations of the consequences of various schemes for multiplication (almost all of which ended in the wastepaper basket). How his symbolic manipulation— all that scribbling—connects with some abstract realm, of which he eventually achieved a factually true description, is a complete mystery. Better to follow Wittgenstein's counsel, and treat Hamilton's activity at face value. With enormous perseverance, Hamilton explored whether a particular set of rules for working with a new notation could be developed into a symbolic game that preserved major features of an established part of mathematics, the algebra and arithmetic of the complex numbers.

The true mathematical statements (or formulae) are those that can be reached by following the rules of a symbolic game—subject, again, to a pragmatic constraint: the game must be one worth playing. Some mathematical games, those belonging to the most elementary parts of mathematics, are worth playing because they help us in coping with pervasive aspects of physical reality. They serve us in collecting, tallying, and distributing objects, and in measuring land. Others permit new ways of systematizing the physical world, or address questions posed in connection with earlier symbolic games, or generalize previous games (as in Hamilton's case), or answer purposes of aesthetic enjoyment, or are fun to play. The sources of mathematical worth turn out to be quite diverse.

Thinking about mathematics in the context of discussing possible refinements of religion is useful, partly because it loosens the grip of thoughts that all truth must be factual, and partly because it points toward a species of truth—ethical truth—refined believers take to be intimately linked to religious truth. Section III distinguished two versions of refined religion, the "straightforward" one that identifies the transcendent as the source of values, and a "modest" alternative that views faith in the transcendent as deepening commitment and confidence with respect to independently grounded values. The difficulty confronting the straightforward version can now be diagnosed more precisely. It arises from conjoining three ideas: ethical truth is factual truth; religion is primarily a commitment to values; the transcendent is unknowable. The second and third of these are crucial to evading the secularist argument of Chapter 1. But when the first is added, refined religion becomes torn: it claims to identify genuine values whose source is apparently unfathomable.

Trouble could be avoided by developing the modest version of refined religion in combination with a constructivist approach to ethical truth, one that regards the truth of value judgments as generated out of particular activities. Constructivism can take several forms. Kantian constructivists liberate Kant's insights from the idea of some prior "realm of reason"; they take something to be valuable (or good, or right) just in case it would be so judged by a subject who reasoned well (in a less exalted sense of cogent reasoning). Or, in a different tradition, the value of something is determined by the status it would be assigned in deliberations among agents negotiating a contract with one another under ideal conditions. Finally, the naturalized account of Chapter 2 identifies correct value judgments as those introduced in progressive transitions in the ethical project, and retained in an indefinitely extended sequence of further progressive transitions.

All three versions share features with my preferred treatment of mathematical truth, most fundamentally in abandoning the assimilation of ethical truth to factual truth. Moreover, like the nonfactual account of mathematical truth, the naturalistic conception of ethical truth incorporates the idea of progressive historical development. In both instances, progress is made by addressing problems appearing in an existing practice, and the truths are the stable elements that survive in an indefinite series of progressive transitions. In the ethical case, the initial problem is posed by the human predicament: we need to live together, but we lack the responsiveness to others to do so smoothly and stably. Progress in the ethical project consists in addressing that problem, as well as the other problems generated from progressive partial solutions. Truth is the distinctive quality of the enduring constituents of ethical progress—"Truth happens to an idea."

I now want to make what may appear to be an absurd claim. Ethical truth is fundamental to all species of truth, factual, mathematical, fictional, religious, or whatever. My claim rests on two suppositions: first, all notions of truth are subject to a pragmatic constraint; second, the pragmatic constraint presupposes a notion of ethical truth.

Section V already introduced the distinction between truth-in-a-language and truth (period), arguing that the latter was subject to the constraint that the language must be apt for the purposes to which it is directed. Subsequent discussions of other modes of truth—fictional, mathematical, ethical—have followed suit in incorporating a pragmatic constraint. Nor is this accidental. Lewis Carroll exposed the basic point in presenting Alice's encounter with Humpty Dumpty, who declares that words shall mean whatever he chooses them to mean. Any of an infinity of potential languages might be used in describing the world, or in playing symbolic games, or in prescribing conduct, but the vast majority of them are Humpty Dumpty languages, of no use or significance in any human project. To talk of truth (period) is to discuss truth in a language worth employing.

Languages are worth employing only when they are apt for realizing some human purpose. But that is too weak to capture the full force of the pragmatic constraint. Purposes themselves can be assessed. A stronger type of aptness does not merely relate languages to what people contingently want to achieve, but to what is *worth* striving for. Ultimately, aptness depends on what human ventures are worth pursuing and on a conception of the good human life, as it emerges from the progressive evolution of the ethical project. Languages worth employing are those answering to valid human purposes.

The validity of a purpose often derives from the fact that achieving the goal will contribute to some more fundamental endeavor. Behind each valid purpose stands a chain of purposes, each more fundamental than its predecessor, culminating in an ultimate purpose. A purpose is valid just in case it is ethically true that its associated ultimate purpose is worthwhile.

Truth depends on the aptness of language. The aptness of language depends on the validity of the purposes the language is to promote. The validity of purposes depends on a claim to ethical truth. Thus, absurd as it may initially sound, ethical truth is fundamental to all species of truth.

VII

The attempt to provide a clear and precise understanding of refined religion has involved taking up topics and questions that are both intricate and also apparently distant from religious matters. The more general examination of modes of truth is, however, necessary for making sense of what champions of refined religion have in mind. They do not simply view religious myths and, more generally, religious declarations as non-literal statements that answer to the contingent ends of particular people in particular situations. Rather, they suppose that religion is "universally fruitful," speaking to the purposes of everyone whose culture progresses sufficiently far. Beside the locally valuable stories stand the enduring myths.

What, exactly, are the purposes religion serves so well? Different refined believers emphasize alternative benefits. Among the favored ends, some candidates recur: religion releases tendencies to joyful experience (James's "fruits for life"), it provides a sense of being "at home in the universe," it enhances fraternity (or, in a more inclusive idiom, social solidarity), and it cultivates ethical sensibility. Elements of this sort provide a start on a concept of religious aptness. Transitions in human practices are religiously progressive when they increase the religious aptness of those practices. In line with the approaches to mathematical truth and ethical truth, a concept of religious truth can now be developed. A statement counts as a religious truth just in case there is a community practice that would make religious progress through affirming the statement, and the affirmation would be preserved in any indefinite sequence of religiously progressive transitions.

Religious truth, so understood, would include mythical truth, but would not be exhausted by it. Religious practices have many dimensions, and statements play other roles besides the telling of stories—public avowals of the faith may, for example, foster a sense of solidarity with others, forging bonds that are needed for struggles to bring about ethically important ends. Nevertheless, considering mythical truth as a special instance of religious truth will focus the central ideas of refined religion.

The apparent confusions discerned in section IV have been resolved. "True myth" is no oxymoron, but simply an appropriate name for religious stories that are religious truths and factual falsehoods. Similarly, "conflicting myths" can be embraced as true, by locating them in communities and traditions to whose practices they are enduringly apt. Whether the embrace should extend to efforts by refined believers to adopt and sincerely affirm all the true myths of all progressive religious traditions is a separate—open—question. Refined religion may be cosmopolitan, attempting to synthesize the religious truths of communities that have historically separated themselves from one another; or it can propose that, while recognizing from the outside the religious truths espoused by others, the fulfilled religious life is best embedded within a specific tradition. Furthermore, versions of refined religion may differ in their assessments of religious progressiveness. Although it extends an ecumenical attitude to all religions, refined religion might not judge all traditions to be equally progressive. Perhaps the notion of religious progress singles out a particular cluster of religions as especially well-developed, for example those initiated roughly three millennia ago (in the "axial age").

The principal substance of any version of refined religion will consist, however, in explaining the elements of the concept of religious aptness and showing how the human purposes singled out are advanced through faith in the transcendent. Substance must be given to the thought that understanding ourselves in relation to something unknowable, toward which the great religious myths only gesture, expands and deepens human experience, making it freer and more joyful. Similarly, refined religion must explain the role of the—metaphorically characterized—transcendent in reconciling us to the cosmos and in forging a sense of solidarity with others (an obvious starting point in accounting for the latter is the metaphor of all human beings as children of a divine parent). I want to conclude my exposition of refined religion, however, by taking up the last of the "enduring human purposes," the enhanced ethical sensitivity of the refined believer, and considering how this goal might be promoted by faith in the transcendent.

The straightforward version of refined religion appears to offer the obvious answer. Values are grounded in the transcendent; hence those who do not acknowledge the transcendent have no hope of discerning what is properly valuable. Seductive though this reasoning may seem, it is undercut by the arguments of Chapter 2 and section III of this chapter. Not only are there alternative explanations of the objectivity of values, but the straightforward version faces severe difficulties in showing how the values it locates in the transcendent can be identified. Although I do not want to write off the straightforward version as definitely incorrect (after all, refined believers might propose convincing responses to the questions I have raised), the modest approach to refined religion appears to be a superior alternative.

Modest refined religion proposes that ethical sensitivity is enhanced by faith in the transcendent because refined believers see their ethical lives in relation to something larger and grander, becoming imbued with deeper commitments and with hope that the ethical ends for which they strive will ultimately be achieved. Surveying the histories of the major religious traditions, refined believers see the great religious teachers (the authors of the Torah and the Gita, the Buddha, the Prophet, Jesus) as inspired by powerful myths, in light of which they transform ethical conversation. Perhaps they have some exceptional understanding of the constructive procedures that ground ethical truth; or, perhaps, they are not final ethical authorities, but proposers, who are able, through their faith, to present new ethical ideas with special passion and vividness. Whether it espouses one of the familiar constructivist accounts of ethical truth (those of the liberal Kantian or the contractualist), or whether (improbably) it adopts the naturalism of Chapter 2, modest refined religion can make a preliminary case for the positive role of faith in ethical life.

To sum up: at least in its modest version, refined religion does not lapse into self-contradiction or confusion or inevitable unclarity. It can articulate conceptions of ethical and religious truth that allow it to escape the secularist arguments of Chapter 1. Moreover, in its initial efforts to specify the enduring purposes that religion—and only religion—can serve it poses challenges secular humanism must address. The final two chapters will take up those challenges.

VIII

First, however, I offer some brief concluding remarks to connect the abstract theses and arguments of earlier sections with contemporary discussions of religion and secularism. Writers sympathetic to religion, typically people who subscribe to some version of refined religion, often charge secularists with telling a simple and historically false story about the growth of their preferred perspective, a "subtraction narrative" in which the progress of Western intellectual and social life has largely consisted in exposing the falsehood of religious claims. According to that story, scientific understanding of nature has gradually beaten back primitive superstitions. Is that an accurate account of what has occurred?

It should no longer be controversial that a Darwinian account of the history of life is a far closer approximation to factual truth than the stories literalists reconstruct from their selective readings of the opening chapters of Genesis. Champions of refined religion are nonetheless right to identify important and pervasive features of human life to which religions have traditionally responded, and thus to challenge the inference from the (correct) premise that substantive religious doctrines are factually false to the conclusion that the ideal future is one in which the amputation of religion proceeds as quickly as possible. Both science and religion might be viewed as progressive, developing factually superior descriptions and explanations as well as enhanced ways of responding to the human condition. Distinguishing factual truth from religious truth allows a clearer appreciation of that possibility.

Contemporary atheists often seem to see only one possible form of religious progress, *purifying progress* as it might well be called. Religions make purifying progress when their practices become so thoroughly disinfected that adherents no longer have the slightest temptation to suppose any doctrinal statement to be factually true. The ideal limit of purifying progress is a religion so refined—a religion from which everything has been "subtracted"—that it withers away into secularism. My aim has been to show how this atheist conception forecloses possibilities, how it neglects other modes of truth besides the factual, and thereby oversimplifies the position of the most thoughtful religious believers. At the root of this widespread form of atheism is, perhaps, a failure to appreciate any pragmatic constraint on truth. Truth is celebrated as an ultimate value, not seen in terms of its promotion of a variety of human ends. In this spirit, those who regret the passing of religious doctrine are supposed to be cheered by the offer of a factually true understanding of aspects of nature. Surely the offer is rewarding—*humanly* rewarding—to those whose lives are centered on participating in scientific discovery, but, for the vast majority of our species, life must be given a different orientation. As Tolstoy's Levin already saw, recognizing the factual truth is not enough.

Yet an important worry underlies the atheist critique. Sophisticated contemporary secularists (like Daniel Dennett) recognize the human purposes religions have traditionally served. Secularists of this stripe emphasize purifying progress as the principal (if not unique) mode of religious progress because they take religious fulfillment of human needs to be insignificant in comparison with the harms of deception and self-deception induced by fuzzy talk about "mythical truth" and "multiple realities." The secularist insight, one that usually slips out of view in the writings of refined believers who celebrate the richness of religious practices, is that nebulous language encourages the breach of boundaries. Even the most refined may glide easily from one species of truth to another. Substantive doctrines, officially denied entry at the front door, slip in through the back. Committed to a connection between values and the transcendent, and convinced of the "deep truth" of a particular myth, believers may derive a new ethical requirement from their preferred scriptures—thereby once again assuming the mantle of authority, supposedly cast off by refined religion, a cloak that has often swathed the ethical project and distorted its shape. Where refined religion celebrates the vividness and passion its favored myths bring to ethical life, secular critics worry that enthusiasm may substitute for reliable processes of ethical deliberation. This chapter has lavished attention on abstract issues precisely because clear boundaries are so important. Without them, we are condemned to interminable debate between cloudy responses to important aspects of life and sharp, but oversimplified, critique.

With the boundaries clearly marked, however, secular humanists and champions of refined religion ought to recognize one another as allies, at least in some battles. Because both acknowledge the falsehood of substantive doctrines, they should band together against people who insist that religion requires belief in specific claims about the transcendent, whether the insistent are advocates for particular substantive doctrines or whether they are critics who take the end of literal doctrine to be the death of religion. Secular humanists ought to admire the refined appreciation of symmetry among religious traditions, hoping that the consequent resolve to view many or all of the world's religions as attempting metaphorical evocations of the same reality is an important step toward ending religious conflict (thus coming to terms with the mutual savagery rightly highlighted in many atheist critiques). Finally, since secular humanism is a positive perspective, one concerned with the value of human lives in a thoroughly natural world, it should benefit from a focus on the right questions, and especially from the presentation of important challenges.

In the end, however, peaceful coexistence must give way to renewed argument. Secularists resist the thought that *only* the myths and practices of religions can address the human condition. To be sure, those elements of religious life have been important to our ancestors. But secular humanists do not see them as irreplaceable or incapable of improvement. Secularists envisage a broadly progressive future, not one in which religion disappears, but one in which it metamorphoses into something else. Proponents of cosmopolitan forms of refined religion take initial steps in this direction, envisaging departures from the main traditions, novel and eclectic syntheses. Secular humanists go much further. They foresee successors to contemporary religious life that draw on a far broader range of cultural items—borrowing from poets and filmmakers, musicians, artists, and scientists, cultivating social institutions to develop the senses of identity and community traditionally fostered by religion. Ancient religious texts may still be read, but their significance will stem from their vivid presentation of some ethical truth, one appreciated independently of any religious claim. The practice will be thoroughly purified. Nobody will suppose that any of the old myths are factually true.

Secular humanists envisage a route to this future that runs through the Enlightenment and the post-Enlightenment past. Refined religion is a way station, not the final destination. Religious believers (and sympathizers) will protest that this is fantasy. Fulfilled human life depends on religion, perhaps in a refined form or perhaps even in more substantial dress. Their protests must now be addressed.

FOUR

MORTALITY AND MEANING

I

In 1868, two years after he had finished the six movements originally planned for his *German Requiem*, Brahms inserted a seventh, a
soprano solo punctuated by muted interjections from the chorus.
The text he chose promises consolation: those who now grieve will
be comforted, the bereaved will again see those they have lost.
Brahms's setting acknowledges the depths of their sorrow, and
responds with gestures of exquisite tenderness. Music-loving secularists, however resolute in their nonbelief, should concede its
emotional power.

Culturally successful religions are often credited with enabling
their followers to understand and to accept the major transitions in
human life. They have, after all, had plenty of practice—typically
centuries or millennia in which they have worked at shaping their
rites. Those, like Christianity and Islam, that promise an eternal continuation to which mundane human life is a prelude, seem especially
adept at coping with the last transition: death is supposedly easier for
the devout to bear. Part of the relief comes from prospects of personal
continuation and hopes for reunion with others who have been loved
and lost. Consoling too is the faith that each finite human existence
connects to something transcendent, and thereby gains an eternal

significance. For the non-believer, however, there is no hope of future survival or of reclaiming the dead. Individual human lives are thoroughly finite, their effects evanescent. *All* human life will eventually cease. Our finitude leaves nothing to celebrate in the wake of a life. What use is Darwin at a funeral?

Mortality and meaning raise connected challenges for secular humanism. On matters of life and death, however, religion offers less, and secularism provides more, than is usually assumed.

II

How should a secular humanist think about the prospect of his own death? A classic recommendation sees fear as inappropriate: with death comes the end of pain, of suffering, of frustrated striving. Hamlet, meditating suicide, calls death "a consummation devoutly to be wished," until, turning suddenly devout, he imagines an afterlife in which the torments of mundane existence continue. Secularists who dismiss that possibility can return to Hamlet's original stance: being dead is nothing to be frightened of.

There is, however, the getting there. Fear can be directed not toward the state itself, but at the process of dying. People are often afraid not only of the pains that come at the end, but also of the unraveling of body and mind, the losses of capacities relied on in their active days. So they are terrified at the thought of what they are likely to become, foreseeing the surviving being as a grotesque parody of themselves. Concerns of this sort are serious, deserving confrontation by the person who contemplates her own life's ending and support from those who might help her avoid, or at least mitigate, the conditions she fears. Support need not—probably should not—come from religion but from humane deployment of medical resources. Careful thoughts about the end should be fostered, expressed, developed in exchanges with those who know about the options, in "end of life" conversations designed to allow the inevitable decaying and dying to approximate a termination suited to her reflective image of her life and her death. Secular humanists regret that religious affiliations, and indeed religious interventions, all too often override people's considered hopes and concerns about the inevitable ending.

Fear of being dead is misplaced, fear of decaying and dying belongs to the anxieties of life, to be addressed with sympathy by whatever techniques of amelioration medical practice can provide. Yet perhaps the concern has been misstated by focusing on the wrong emotion. As you look forward to the future, to a world without you, you might feel regret, rather than fear, being sad that you will no longer be a part of the show. There might be psychological pain, even quite acute, at the prospect of your nonexistence. Again, there is a classic reassurance, stemming from the ancient world. As you look back into the past, you contemplate with equanimity the long expanses of time before you were born. No pangs disturb you as you think about your absence from particular historical episodes. Why then should you feel any differently about the future?

So far I've offered a swift review of familiar attempts at secular consolation. If they constitute a *beginning*, they do not go far in addressing the root anxieties—many people regard them as facile, shallow, even as laughable sophistry. The sorrow or repugnance felt in contemplating a future from which you will be absent is not to be assimilated to everyday reactions to pain and suffering. It is deeper, an emotion of distress, or even terror, at the prospect that you will no longer be. To help bring this reaction into sharper focus, I shall replace the classical query about past and future with a different question: Do you feel differently about your absence from different parts of the future?

I do. As I imagine the world in the years *immediately* following my death, I feel a more intense regret about not being part of it than when I project forward a century, or even half a century. Increasing the time interval diminishes my sadness—it fades relatively swiftly to indifference. Not because I'm envious of those who live happily and actively into extreme old age. I don't even yearn for the longevity advances in medicine may someday achieve for future generations. Absence from the period just after my death is poignant because so much of the stuff of my life will be continued in it. *Whenever* I die, people about whom I care most deeply will live on, and I should like to be there, sustaining them and being sustained by them. Endeavors to which I have committed my energies will remain unfinished. Loose ends will be left, and I should like to tie them up—while knowing that ends are always beginnings and strands will inevitably dangle. By contrast, the connections with the more distant future are dim, and I cannot even be confident of the large contours of the remote world from which I shall be excluded. Were I to survive into that world, there would be a continuously evolving set of relationships and activities that would give me a stake in it, but, lacking any experience of that development of my life, the concerns I would come to have are not vivid for me. So, as I look forward sufficiently far, regret declines into indifference.

Those who shudder at the thought of their nonexistence in *any* part of the future will see this reaction as only a slight improvement on the ancient idea that past and future can be contemplated with equal serenity. In this area of my thought and feeling, I shall appear to them as akin to the color-blind and the tone-deaf. But what are the analogues of the hues and pitches that normal people can differentiate? What contrasts with absence from the future? What envisaged state would *not* provoke the shudder?

World literature tells of many people who react to the prospect of death by longing for immortality, and of some among them whose wish is granted. The incautious ones—Tithonus, for example—forget to ask that vigor, youth, and beauty should be part of the bargain. Tennyson captures their lament:

Me only cruel immortality
Consumes: I wither slowly in thine arms, . . .

But this, you may think, is a technicality. What is really desirable is the possibility of living forever at the height of your powers—or, perhaps, the possibility of living forever with the option of assuming, at any moment in time, whatever life-stage you choose—and it is the realization that these possibilities are denied us that causes distress or terror.

Tennyson's Tithonus makes a deeper point, however, when he regrets his deviation from the *happiness* of the finite human lot. Ensuring eternal vigor (or permanent options for choosing your age) abstracts from some conditions of human life, but it does not modify a fundamental aspect of human finitude. For each of us, there is a number of ways in which we might choose to lead our lives. Perhaps it is a very large number—but it is not infinite. If you imagine your immortality in concrete detail, it would decompose into a sequence of episodes. Rather than having a single coherent narrative arc, it would be a loose picaresque novel or a disjointed collection of short stories—however fulfilling the individual episodes might be, it would be hard to understand the whole as *a* life. Furthermore, it would reach a point when immortality became tedious and burdensome, not because your powers had withered but because there was nothing new under the sun. Tired of attempts to develop infinite variations on finite material, weary of repetition, like Tithonus you would long to rejoin the mortal human condition.

We cannot, I think, fully imagine what it would be like to be the kind of being for which immortality was a condition of eternal joy. If my diagnosis is correct, distress at the prospect of not being is founded in a confusion. For absence from *any* part of the future is only terrible because something is felt as having been lost. If extended sufficiently far, however, *human* lives would not be vulnerable to any real loss through the threat of termination—indeed, cessation would ultimately appear as a blessing. What lies behind the sense of horror at not being is regret at being human. To my humanist sensibility that species of regret appears one we should try to overcome—just as we should seek to accept, even enjoy, the arc of our aging. Our real problem is posed by the prospect of a removal from a web of connections that matter deeply to us.

The loss of the immediate future is hard for those whose lives attain, or approach, the biblically allotted span, but for the young who face the threat of imminent death the sorrow is even more intense. No member of their unfortunate ranks has expressed the predicament more eloquently than Keats:

> When I have fears that I may cease to be
> Before my pen has glean'd my teeming brain,
> Before high pilèd books, in charact'ry
> Hold like rich garners the full-ripened grain; . . .

Regret and sadness become fear, but the fear is not of death in general—that is nothing to be frightened of. *Premature* death, however, is fearsome, even terrifying, because it truncates and nullifies the pattern of a life. Although the later lines of the sonnet worry that he will never experience the love for which he yearns, Keats's first anxiety is for the expression of his genius. Central to his existence is his poetic vocation. If that vocation were realized only in a mutilated, abbreviated form, the meaning of his life would be lost.

Following Keats, I take the genuine problem of death to be the problem of premature death. Deaths count as premature when they prevent lives from attaining meaning: the challenges of mortality and meaning connect. But aren't all deaths premature? Can any finite life be meaningful?

III

A proposal: human lives sometimes attain meaning through individuals' developing conceptions of who they are and what matters to their existences, through their pursuit of the goals endorsed by those conceptions, and by some degree of success in attaining them. A Keats who lived for eighty years, piling up books full of poetry as extraordinary as the lyrics he wrote at the height of his powers, would have led a meaningful life, whether or not he found love along the way. Indeed, the actual Keats, leaving only a fraction of what he might have written, lived a life whose meaning is untouched by his early death. Nor is exceptional achievement needed. Secularists should endorse not only the grand accomplishments of the poets and the statesmen and the scientists, but also the humbler self-conceptions of those whose pursuits and achievements focus more locally, on family, on friendship, on community, on the maintenance of things that matter to a small group of other people.

Mattering to others is what counts in conferring meaning. Keats matters to others because of the body of verse that continues to delight. The effects of more ordinary lives are felt on a smaller scale, but they still secure genuine worth. The nature of the dispute between religious and secular perspectives should now be visible. For the religious challenger, no set of characteristics of finite lives, or of relations among finite lives, can substitute for the connection to the transcendent that alone confers meaning and value.

Problems about our own deaths lead to deeper issues about the significance of finite lives. Yet the thought that *we* shall cease to be is not the only way death figures as a problem for us. The loss of loved ones lacks secular compensation. In the beginning the fabric of a human life is tightly woven. All the threads tying us together are fully intact. As people grow, however, holes appear, leaving frayed ends that cannot be reconnected. For those who live the longest, the final tapestry is a thing of shreds and tatters, its yawning vacancies recalling people whose laughter and whose touch is still longed for. Growing old beside someone you love brings the overwhelmingly likely prospect of an ending in which one will mourn the loss of the other, and the inevitable shrinking of the survivor's life is—for both parties—more fearsome than the anticipation of one's own bodily and mental decay.

Back, then, to Brahms and the promise of reunion. Here apparently is a consolation secular humanism cannot match, a hope religious widows and widowers sometimes confess they could not forfeit. Well-meaning people occasionally tender a similar hope to those who grieve for children who have died young—as Charles Kingsley did in a letter to his friend Thomas Henry Huxley. Huxley had lost his beloved first son, Noel, at the age of four, and Kingsley (the reverend Charles Kingsley) regretted that the celebrated agnostic (Huxley had even invented the term) could not look forward to a reunion with the boy in the hereafter. Despite his grief, Huxley responded with an unflinching declaration of his resolve to "serve Truth."

Imagine for a moment that Kingsley's vision of the hereafter was correct. Would his promise of a future meeting have answered to what his friend so desperately wanted? I think not. No such reunion would have extended the threads death had broken. Huxley's life had been interwoven with that of the child—he had anticipated guiding the boy through his formative years, watching him mature into an adult, gradually fashioning a new, more equal, relationship with Noel, looking on as the young man created his own pattern for his life. Parents who have lost their children, lovers who mourn the beloved, people who miss a close friend want a continuation in the here and now, not a meeting under very different, dimly imaginable conditions in which two strangers, whose lives are no longer connected, confront one another. The hole in life's fabric demands immediate repair.

The religious challenger is likely to protest that the dismissal of the promised comfort rests on misunderstanding the character of the afterlife, on substituting a crude vision that undermines the real consolation. Yet mistaken as they may be about the glories of the hereafter, the bereaved are surely clear about the aching gap they feel in their lives. Whatever happens in the future, there is a loss in the mundane present. Moreover, refined religion, with its abstract, indescribable transcendent, cannot deliver reassurance. For Kingsley's hope, or anything similar, to respond in any fashion to the sorrows of the bereaved it must rest on substantive religious doctrines: the words Brahms set must be heard as importing the everyday implications of *"Wiedersehen."* Although Christians often express disdain for the material comforts of the paradise the Qur'an holds out to Muslims, the Islamic vision has the merit of connecting with the desires of the faithful. When religion retreats to confessing that the transcendent is a mystery, only apprehensible through figurative suggestions, its advertised power to bring comfort in the wake of death dissolves. Huxley was right to suppose that what crumbs of comfort Kingsley offered depended on swallowing a fiction—on accepting dubious articles of specific doctrine, and thus forsaking his devotion to factual truth.

Is this too harsh? The modest version of refined religion takes faith in the transcendent to provide a basis for hope that important values can be realized. Were Kingsley to speak in this idiom, he might claim that the development of loving relationships (between, for example, parents and children) has a place among the important values, so that, without violating Huxley's admirable principles, refined faith could provide him with hope. But to respond in this way would be to slide across one of the boundaries the previous chapter aimed to draw. Realization of the value of parental love need by no means take the highly specific form of reunion in the hereafter—a secular realization would be an enduring tenderness for Noel, preserved in Huxley's memories of the boy. Without compromising itself, refined religion cannot provide any basis for hope that those we have lost will ultimately be found again.

Although the impotence of refined religion is clearer in the case of those who mourn, analogous issues arise in contemplating one's own death. First, whatever the qualities of the envisaged continuation, present losses remain: projects, some of them important, are left unfinished. If the compensation offered is a life in which suffering is behind us, in which there is an end to challenges and an end to struggle, the promise has a superficial appeal—but only until we reflect that our individual identities are founded in commitments, in goals we struggle to realize, that glorifying a form of existence in which all our strivings cease nullifies what we do and who we are. We may envisage a being psychologically continuous with ourselves, no longer invested in anything we have taken to be significant or central, but it is hard to regard that being as anyone we would want to become or to celebrate its existence as a splendid continuation of our own. Further, even this relatively abstract conception of the afterlife, characterized by the psychological continuation of persons in circumstances from which suffering and challenge have been removed, depends on a modestly literal reading of a phrase from Whittier, set in a famous hymn: in God's presence, "all our strivings cease." Refined religion cannot assume so much, and its restrained conception of the transcendent offers no basis for supposing an afterlife in which any being remotely like any of us has a presence.

In the end, any additional comforts religion offers depend on ignoring the arguments of Chapter 1, and settling for substantive doctrines that are almost certainly false. Refined religion provides nothing superior to what secular humanism can offer. Yet a fall into unrefined religion fails to touch many aspects of what we feel in the face of death. Gibes about Darwin's uselessness at funerals misunderstand the human situation. Death should usually be an occasion for sorrow, often one for anguish, on any religious or any secular account—for whatever dubious comfort is promised for a conjectural future, the torn fabric of mundane life remains unrepaired. If Brahms's soprano uplifts her hearers for a moment, if she brings them consolation, that is because the music she sings is beautiful and its sensitivity to the words reminds us vividly of things that are rightly loved and valued *within human life*. The real challenges focus on meaning and finitude. The problem is not whether secularists can match the religious response to death, but whether they can make adequate sense of life.

IV

The question of the good life is the oldest issue of Western philosophy, one that drew the privileged young men of the ancient world to the various philosophical schools. Their mentors instructed them in alternative techniques for living well: learn and practice virtue, be active in political life, cultivate friendships, pursue knowledge for its own sake, limit pleasures to those maintaining psychological equilibrium, and so forth. Contemporary judgment might expand the ancient catalogue, and undo the distortions imposed by conceiving the good life as possible only for a privileged elite. After the fall of Rome, however, the old philosophical question lapsed in the intellectual culture of the West, for it seemed to have received a definitive solution. The Christian churches declared that the valuable life is one directed toward God, centered on obedience to God's commandments, and rewarded by an eternal continuation. The finite span allotted to us on earth is only a prelude, its worth determined by whether it fits us for eternity.

The Enlightenment brought a detached appraisal of the religious solution, and revived interest in the ancient problem. Secular thinkers returned to considering how people might best spend the years between birth and death, endorsing the importance of many of the qualities highlighted in the classical tradition. Reacting against a prominent feature of the religious conception of the meaningful life, the outside imposition of meaning on the individual, some thinkers—Kant, Humboldt, and Mill notable among them—emphasized the importance of autonomy. Because any human life is the life of a particular person, it should express an individually chosen pattern. For a life to be meaningful, the person must have some conception of who she is and what aspirations are most important, and this conception must not be imposed from without. In Mill's classic formulation, the highest form of freedom is to "pursue one's own good in one's own way."

So the ancient problem is reconfigured. Each meaningful life is distinguished by a theme, a conception of the self and a concomitant identification of the goals it is most important to pursue. That theme should be autonomously chosen by the person whose life it is. But we ought not overinterpret talk of "themes" and "autonomous choice." Meaningful lives are not restricted to the privileged few, to an elite of the high-minded. Autonomous choice of life theme does not require a transformative event, an epiphany around sixteen, say, when a condition of detached freedom permits the review of a large range of options and identification with exactly one of them, in a commitment never to be amended or revoked. Someone's life theme may not be formulated explicitly, unless or until a questioner inquires what matters most to her. Her autonomy may consist in the presence of different possibilities, intermittently recognized as available, and in the absence of the everyday ways in which people are often coerced into assuming the tasks and roles that dominate their lives. Moreover the theme itself may evolve under the contingent conditions generated from previous pursuits: originally centered on nurturing her children, a mother bears an infant who needs a particular kind of help to grow to independence, and, through learning how to provide the necessary support, she comes to play a far broader role in assisting similar children.

Are there further constraints on life themes beyond the requirement that the choice of them be autonomous? The Enlightenment thinkers who returned to the ancient question believed there were, casting the classical emphasis on virtue as the demand that themes be ethically permissible. Mill limits his fundamental form of freedom: one person's choices and pursuits of his own good must not interfere with the counterpart choices and pursuits of others. The constraint should be accepted, but it is too weak. Many projects posing no threat to the life patterns and the lives of others would be insignificant and worthless. Imagine, for example, an asocial solitary, retreating to some remote place and passing his days in counting the blades of grass growing in the vicinity. Lives like that are wasted. So too, as

I'll contend later, are others, all too common in the affluent world, in which people center their lives on the pursuit of wealth and material possessions, their self-conception summed up in a bumper sticker: "He who dies with the most toys wins."

Lives matter when they touch others. The problem of limited responsiveness was and remains the center of ethical practice, and individual lives gain meaning through their own contributions to solving that problem, through actions prompted by recognizing what other people want or need and attempting to provide the things required. Ethical values are social creations, worked out collectively to address a basic problem of the human situation (as well as to tackle further problems that arise in the history of partial solutions). The meanings of lives are individual creations, products of people's autonomous choices, but framed always by the core ethical ideal of other-directedness.

Is there then no place for the meaningful life founded on the development of special talent, of genius that recognizes itself and dedicates itself to self-expression? Indeed there is. For the demand of other-directedness is met if talent and expressed genius are to be worthy of the names. Keats's fears of death as truncating the expression of his genius already presupposed a connection between what he hoped to write and the lives of others, made concrete in the vision of "high pilèd books" as granaries to nourish his readers. If his writings had failed to move or illuminate others, or if he had been resolved that his verse should be confined to his "teeming brain," his choice of theme could not have conferred meaning on his brief life.

Some lives are meaningful because their effects endure across many generations, perhaps in the form of words that continue to be read with profit or joy, perhaps in the guise of material objects or institutional structures, enriching the lives of many people who, when they occasionally think about them, are grateful for what they have inherited. The great touch the lives of millions or billions, of people remote and unknown to them—as Diotima once told Socrates, they have the best kinds of children. Yet, it is important to reject exceptionalism, the modern counterpart of ancient elitism. Ordinary lives attain meaning in the more local, but no less important, differences they make. Ambitious young Stephen Dedalus avows his resolve to "forge in the smithy of my soul the uncreated conscience of my race." Joyce reintroduces him once his attempt to soar high has led him to share the fate of Icarus, his classical counterpart, setting him beside a different protagonist, Mr Leopold Bloom, advertising canvasser, whose ordinary life, for all its blotches and flaws, may yet attain worth and meaning.

Religious people might concede that the features I have focused on mark differences among human lives, while denying that they can confer meaning. Detached from any connection to the transcendent, these features, however richly present, are always insufficient. Secular lives may be better or worse—health is better than sickness, generous attempts to help others superior to inward-turning misanthropy—but the everyday qualities and virtues always fall short of genuine significance. Autonomy matters when, and only when, it expresses the free commitment to the transcendent; contributing to the lives of others is transformed when human beings are understood (metaphorically) as children of a common parent. Without filiations to something transcending human life, no amount of the qualities secularists prize could achieve real significance. No link to the transcendent, no meaning.

Fear of finitude runs through the writings of religious thinkers as sophisticated as William James and Paul Tillich. They regard the "problem of finitude" as dooming any nonreligious perspective. Similar anxieties sometimes infect secular pessimists too, leading them to infer from the bounded impact of any human existence to the absurdity of life. Pessimism is vividly encapsulated in James's haunting image of our predicament: we are like "people living on a frozen lake, surrounded by cliffs over which there is no escape," fully aware that the ice is slowly melting and that the day on which they will vanish without trace is drawing ever closer. Religion is the answer to their—to our—cry for help.

Nobody should deny that the human span, individual and collective, is finite. Nor is it controversial that reflection on this fact can prove disconcerting. The issue is whether that undermines the meaning and value of any human life, even lives that, by secular lights, go well.

V

Why should impermanence cancel meaning? We can counter James's image with a different story. In *Doktor Faustus*, Thomas Mann's protagonist, the composer Adrian Leverkühn, experiences two deaths in close proximity. In Buchel, Leverkühn's childhood home, his father dies. The composer has taken up residence in a different region of Germany, on another farm with an eerie resemblance to the surroundings of his early years. Max Schweigestill, the owner of that farm and the counterpart of his biological father, dies at about the same time as the elder Leverkühn. Adrian's health is not robust enough for him to make the long journey back to Buchel, but he does attend the ceremony for Schweigestill. Returning from the funeral, he is greeted by the distinctive smell of the old man's pipe.

> "That endures," said Adrian. "Quite a while, perhaps as long as the house stands. It lingers on in Buchel too. The period of our lingering afterwards, perhaps a little shorter or a little longer, that is what is called immortality."

The ordinary unpretentious endurance of Max Schweigestill is partly captured in the aroma, impregnated in the woodwork and the walls of the house in which he has passed his entire life.

Eventually, of course, the odor will dissipate, the farm will be tended and maintained by people who know Max Schweigestill only as a figure in faded photographs, the walls and fences he built will decay and be replaced, the fields he plowed and planted will be newly configured and put to different uses. For a while, though, he will be vivid in the memories of those who knew him, who were sustained by his labors and comforted by his presence. The fabric of their lives, initially left ragged by his death, will be rewoven in ways that preserve and cherish the recollections. His commitment to maintain and improve the farm his father left him, and to pass it on to his own son, will be felt in the early years after his death. So much, Mann invites us to think, perhaps stretching the concept too far, suffices for a kind of immortality. Whether or not we acquiesce in his choice of words, this "lingering" is enough to confer meaning on an ordinary life.

Would there be some qualitative difference if the impact of Schweigestill's life were considerably extended, if his achievements were as long-lived as those of Keats, or even, implausibly, if his agricultural accomplishments were recalled across the millennia as we celebrate the Homeric epics? Would the significance of his life be transformed if we imagined the earth and the human species and the farm and the memories of Max Schweigestill to last forever? I think not. What matters is the fact that this life has a continuing connection to a world that endures beyond it. Like a stone cast into a pool, it leaves a series of ripples behind, sometimes more, sometimes less, and it doesn't matter that the ripples eventually fade away.

Conceiving meaning in this way allows a more complete answer to the problems posed by death. Corresponding to the anguish of premature death is the consolation of the fulfilled life. The truly lucky are those who can come to see that the projects singled out in their life themes have been largely finished—not completely, of course, for there are always further endeavors, always loose ends. While they may take their current strivings seriously, and hope for the joys brought when those strivings are successful, reflection may convince them that they have done enough, that if life ended now it would not disrupt or subvert their most fundamental aspirations. A New Testament story captures the attitude beautifully. When the baby Jesus is brought to the Temple to be circumcised, he is seen and held by the aged Simeon, prompting the declaration Anglican choirs sing as the *Nunc Dimittis:* "Lord, now lettest thou thy servant depart in peace, according to thy word, For mine eyes have seen thy salvation. . . ." Simeon's reaction can be liberated from the specifically divine project he takes to have been realized; it can be felt by anyone who recognizes that enough has been done to elaborate his life theme. Purely mundane life might bring a point where "all our strivings cease," where the gains in bringing further projects to successful conclusion add less and less to what has already been accomplished. Drawing inspiration from a different text, we can recognize the fortunate possibility of accepting serenely the ending of one's revels—there can be calm and comfort in supposing that a human life, a "little life," is "rounded with a sleep." Especially if Prospero's lines are read with the emphasis on "rounded," they point to fulfillment, to a conclusion in which what was sought has been found, what was striven for achieved. So, like Simeon, Prospero (and perhaps his creator as well) can show us how finitude can be embraced.

Thoughts of an indefinitely extending future promise only repetitions whose significance fades to nothingness—even a long finite continuation would wither into triviality. As I suggested earlier, human finitude is expressed in the fact that we lack the capacity for playing infinite variations on the narrative of our lives. If it were protracted, the fulfilled human life would eventually have to strike out in some new direction, pursuing a novel theme. Extended, the life would tack on to its original coherence some different venture, one that might, with luck, be equally "rounded." Occasionally, actual human lives do seem to consist of two or three stylistically different acts, each of which resolves itself in successful concord. Life themes can develop and the attainment of new goals can follow achievement of the older ones. Yet lives of this varied sort are neither more nor less meaningful than those that pursue a single course, that complete one satisfying narrative arc. Why then should it be supposed that a finite sequence of different fulfilled lives would be superior to a single one, that if Simeon could go on to a second career as Prospero and a third as Shakespeare, that would constitute an improvement? Beyond the finite sequence lies only the exhaustion of potential choices, and eventually the weary staleness of repetition, the plaints of Tithonus and of Elina Makropulos. The fortunate can be prepared for an exit, a well-timed departure. They are aware of the tedium of any form of immortality beyond that Mann's Leverkühn assigned to Schweigestill.

Those left behind cannot feel the same equanimity. How could they? They have lost a person whom they still long to see and touch and hear. Yet, provided they have time to renew and refashion their own life patterns, their awareness of the fulfilled life enables them to integrate the memories of the dead into their continuing relationships and endeavors. Eventually other people will occupy the spaces originally left achingly blank. Nor will the new loves constitute a betrayal, for they will be recognized as shaped by memories of those once mourned, the dead, no longer recalled with such keen anguish but remembered with something akin to reverence.

Demanding that genuinely meaningful lives should "transcend finitude" is a common trope—but, for all that, a prejudice. What stands behind the thought that nothing we do makes a significant impact unless its effects are permanent? Not the force of some yearning that naturally and inevitably wells up when the prospect of eternal propagation of effects comes into view—for, insofar as that future can be envisaged, it has no real connection with what people aspire to be and to achieve, and consequently no particular attraction. Perhaps, then, the source of insistence on overcoming finitude is an argument. My life could obtain meaning from its effect on other lives only if those other lives themselves were meaningful. Supposing meaning to accrue from mattering to others begins a regress: the other lives would obtain their meaning from their impact on yet further lives, whose meaning-fulness would depend on their effects on yet more remote people, and so on and on. Because the sequence cannot proceed indefinitely—human life will eventually cease and all James's ice-dwellers will be drowned—there must be some last member of the chain. Since this person can have no impact on some subsequent meaningful life, her life is deprived of meaning. Lack of meaning now seeps backward through the entire sequence: because those in the $(n + 1)$st place do not enjoy meaningful lives, the people at the nth stage do not have effects on meaningful lives, and hence their lives are devoid of meaning.

Stating the argument explicitly makes it evident how to resist it. The picture of something acquiring meaning through relationship to something else that already has meaning is doomed from the start, especially if the somethings are qualitatively akin. But we can reject that picture in favor of taking meaning to lie in the relationship itself. One life may be meaningful through its attempts to affect the lives of others, efforts that contribute to the possibility of the lives affected developing meaningfully, even though contingent factors subvert that development. Schweigestill's life would remain meaningful even if the fortunes of family and farm gradually declined across the subsequent generations, even if the property were eventually sold and the descendants scattered in a very different society. Nothing human endures forever, but lives centered on trying to extend the existence of something people treasure are not automatically deprived of meaning by the fact of impermanence.

Refined religion sets against this image of meaningful lives with local, short-lived effects an ostensibly grander perspective. Independent of human aspirations there is some eternal goal, and the meaning of individual lives stems from their acquiescence in the goal and the—necessarily infinitesimal—contributions people make to it. Transcending finitude is purchased at the cost of autonomy. Mill's "fundamental freedom," the choice of one's own good, is subordinated to a cosmic enterprise beyond human understanding; our autonomy is reduced to acceptance of a remote venture in which we are to play bit parts, without any clear consciousness of how our doings contribute. We are minute cogs in a vast machine whose point exceeds our comprehension. How our condition of alienated labor confers meaning on what we do must remain a mystery. Worse still, the ordinary things that matter to people, the stuff of meaningful lives, do not receive their value from any human concerns: relations to the lives of others are not significant because extending and expanding responsiveness is at the heart of ethical life. Rather acts of caring, nurturing, sustaining, and protecting achieve their special status from the terms of the cosmic enterprise. The yearning to transcend human finitude ends by restricting autonomy and estranging what is most centrally human.

Meaningful lives do require a connection to something larger, but not to anything eternal or cosmic. Humanism affirms both the potential meaningfulness of our deeds and the finite character of their impact, endorsing the "enduring," the "local immortality," recalled by Mann's protagonist. In this sense, humanism can only be secular.

VI

Once clearly in view, the intellectual problems posed for secular humanism by mortality and meaning can be resolved. Practical difficulties, however, remain.

Many, probably most, human lives do not go well. Among the contemporary global population, millions, if not billions, struggle to gather the necessities that enable them, and their children, to continue from day to day. For many more, secularist praise of autonomous choice of "one's own good" could only be heard as a tasteless joke. Statistics indicate that religious adherence and religious fervor flourish among the people most vulnerable to the vicissitudes of life. That should be no surprise, for religious doctrine and religious community can provide hope that the reversals of the present fragile existence will somehow be compensated. They can also create opportunities for mutual support and consolation. Even if, under scrutiny, the promises of future rewards turn out to be hollow, the benefits brought by religious community may be real.

Because substantive religious doctrines often retain the prejudices inscribed by the supposed ethical authorities of the tradition—for example in their views of the roles appropriate for women—they can intensify the confinement of autonomy and erect further barriers to the realization of a meaningful life. Nevertheless, religious communities have often played an important role in bringing the powerless together, identifying shared sources of oppression, and combining voices so a chorus of complaint can at last be heard. Famously, the civil rights movement of the 1960s was grounded in the churches, and led by eloquent preachers who could galvanize their congregations. Less evident to many, although not to those who have first-hand experience of contemporary urban poverty, is the social role religious communities continue to provide, the resources they offer to families struggling to create better opportunities for their children in environments where secular institutions are woefully inadequate and where the temptation to acquiesce in hopelessness is omnipresent.

It does not have to be that way. Secular society might respond to the problems of economic and social justice, honoring the egalitarian ideal of the provision for all of the preconditions for a meaningful life. Even the most striking attempts to nurture all nascent lives, undertaken in Scandinavian societies, have fallen short of the ideal. The lapses of other affluent countries, in northern Europe, or in Japan, in Canada, Australia, Britain, and the United States are successively more glaring, signifying at the latter end of the continuum a willingness to treat many lives as effectively disposable. On a global scale, however, the predicament is even worse. Central to the normative stance of Chapter 2 is a commitment to socioeconomic justice across the human species. Beyond declaring abstract rights we should demand that the world's resources be shared so as to allow to all people (or, more exactly, to all people except those whose biological limitations cannot be overcome) the opportunity for a meaningful life.

However thorough the dedication to egalitarian ideals, there will always be lives that do not go well—lives disrupted by contingencies beyond prediction or control. There will be no utopia in which all people enjoy the good life to which the aristocrats of the ancient world aspired. But we can try to decrease the frequency at which human lives fall short—indeed to decrease it dramatically. When lives go awry, there should be efforts at rescue, support for the person's search for a new direction. If the efforts fail, that is a genuine loss, not to be glossed over with false promises of some future compensation. This is the only life the person has. We should be committed to salvage, not to salvation.

Literalist religions often do better than secular institutions in responding to the conditions dooming many people to lives marked by insecurity and confined to narrow horizons. But their efforts are compromised by supposing present failures to be redeemed in the hereafter, by affirming doctrines tainted by traditional prejudices, and by commitments to exclusivity. The eternal reward awaiting those who have suffered is wonderful enough to justify extreme measures for ensuring that all meet the conditions required to receive it. Doctrines that seduce people from the true path must be resisted; those who uphold the deviant doctrines must be fought with every available weapon. The soil that nourishes consolation for the downtrodden also supports the growth of a noxious weed—violent religious strife—that intensifies the material and social miseries.

Religions that refine the pertinent elements, abandoning any literal commitment to immortality and the traditional divisive prejudices, do not offer the concrete promise, but they often do far better in reshaping the lives of the unfortunate. Secular humanists can reasonably see refined believers as allies in an ethically fundamental enterprise, co-campaigners whose currently greater successes make them worthy targets of emulation.

Thinking of religions and religious communities as only directed toward the plight of the needy and oppressed misses an important dimension of the work they do. Connection to others is central to the meaningful life, but so far I have emphasized the simplest form of connection, pairwise relations between individuals. Most meaningful lives exhibit a more complex structure of affiliations. Engaging with many others in joint projects and sharing purposes is central to their life themes—it is important to participate in common endeavors, that the endeavors proceed through mutual responsiveness, and that the people themselves contribute to the eventual outcome. Today most of us belong to societies in which the web of associations is not simply given, as it once was for our Paleolithic ancestors or for the closely knit villages of the pre-industrial world. Contemporary people must seek community. Religious institutions are often the only places in which they can find it. At their best, their rituals foster responsiveness to others, the public avowal of prayer becoming a stimulus to joint ethical deliberation, rather than one side of a dialogue with some transcendent figure.

Communities of believers connect their members, providing a sense of belonging and of being together with others, of sharing problems and of working cooperatively to find solutions. Religious involvement does not merely provide occasions for talk about important issues—although that itself is valuable—but also for joint action. Sharing a religion, whether literalist or refined, can foster agreement on goals, not necessarily focused on the liberation or socioeconomic progress of the faithful. Engaging in common pursuit of a good endorsed by fellow strivers, and doing one's part in the shared effort, can be the source of the deepest satisfactions.

Where are similar satisfactions to be found? Particularly at some life stages, in the narrower circle of the family, in nurturing children and caring for loved ones. In developing individual friendships, and especially in sustaining friends through times of adversity. Typically the spaces in which rewarding interrelations are found are disjoint from the places in which people work, their spheres of most intense activity. To be sure, nurses and teachers, doctors and social workers can participate daily in joint efforts aimed at goals they and their co-workers endorse as important. Research scientists and statesmen may see themselves as cooperating with others to improve the lot of millions. Yet the dominant condition of the workers of the modern world, even of the modern affluent world, is the one Marx diagnosed as alienated labor. The hours must be put in, not to reach any end assessed as worthwhile, by oneself or by one's fellows, but simply so that something will be produced to make enough money to pay the wages and support the material basis of the workers' lives.

Religion does not have to be the main vehicle of community life. Thoroughly secular societies can contain structures enabling people to enter into sympathetic relations with one another, to achieve solidarity with their fellows, to exchange views about topics that concern them most, to work together to identify goals that matter to all members of the group and to pursue those ends through cooperative efforts. Authors of contemporary manifestos calling for freedom from religious delusions typically belong to professional communities with the important dimensions—taking that for granted, the lack of similar *secular* structures for others disappears from their view. Focused on adding to the stock of factual truths, and finding an entirely reasonable satisfaction in sharing that goal with their closest colleagues, they want the delight of apprehending factual truth to be shared by all—just as some devout people hope that all will enjoy the bliss of eternal life—and so they see purifying progress, the replacement of factually false religious doctrines with clear-headed denial, as a major advance for humanity. In many parts of the affluent world, however, particularly in the United States, there are no serious opportunities, outside the synagogues and churches and mosques, for fellowship with all the dimensions religious communities can provide. Perhaps among small groups of friends there are occasional moments at which serious discussion becomes possible, when aspirations can be revealed or doubts confessed, when what might be worth doing can be patiently explored. In most secular settings, however, such explorations would be an embarrassment. So the necessary words go unspoken, the spread of sympathy into others' lives is checked, goals are decided and pursued largely alone. The actual secular world thus forfeits the most significant aspects of community life. Purifying progress leaves many erstwhile believers exposed to the chill of a lonely and inhospitable world.

By contrast, some people who have little time for any substantive religious doctrine view the persistence of religion in the modern world as a welcome corrective to the dominance of crass materialism. Their diagnosis rests on an important insight, despite the fact that it is usually presented in terms of preserving the "spiritual" aspects of our nature. The core perception recognizes the conditions of modern life as distorting the autonomous choice and pursuit of "one's own good," diverting people from more meaningful forms of existence they might have pursued and enjoyed. Satisfaction of the material needs of all, the preconditions of affording opportunities for meaningful lives, generates the quest for efficient production and the unsparing competition of the workplace. The secondary goal trickles down to individual lives, now seen as competing for material goods and for the marks of status. Atomistic individuals attempt to play *Homo economicus*, not a role for which human beings are particularly well suited. Family life provides some refuge for meaningful projects—although these too may be misshapen by the assumption that the young must above all be equipped for the competition to come (the rat race begins in the cradle, or even earlier). Beyond the family projects lie only the goals of accumulating goods and prestige and of enjoying evanescent pleasures—goals the ancients already knew to be inadequate aspirations for a flourishing life. Religion is rightly seen as a corrective to the materialism of the age, not because it draws attention to any real "spiritual realm," nor because of the correctness of any specific religious doctrine (no matter how minimal), nor because religion is the source of values, but because of the importance to us of a multidimensional form of community life. For large swaths of contemporary affluent societies, that form of shared ethical life is in short supply, and religious communities are the principal places in which it can be found.

Secular humanism faces no *intellectual* problems in accounting for the potential meaningfulness of human existence. The real difficulties are practical, grounded in the need to overcome aspects of the contemporary world that unnecessarily limit the lives of many people. Resolving them is, in part, a matter of rethinking economic life and institutions, returning to a conception of political economy that frames its standards in the fundamental currency of values, not in the secondary goals of monetary profit. A central task is to devise secular substitutes for the multidimensional community life religions have been able to bestow on their followers. Attempts to solve that problem may seek inspiration in the successful strategies of the world's religions—as the most prominent ventures in fashioning secular community, Unitarian churches, Societies for Ethical Culture, and Jewish Community Centers have all done. If the initial results seem pallid imitations of the religious prototypes, lacking the powerful rites with their resonant words and uplifting music, it is worth recalling that the religions have had centuries of practice. Humanists, as well as critics who think a secular perspective cannot suffice, should remember that experiments require time to make them work, and should pursue the important practical goal with perseverance and patience.

FIVE

DEPTH AND DEPRAVITY

I

In Tolstoy's fictional presentation of his own doubts and torments, Levin protests the impossibility of living by the science of his day. Demanding protection against the chill of a purely secular perspective, he finds it in returning to religion. During the hundred and forty years since the writing of *Anna Karenina*, many people have surely gone a distance with Levin, some of them overcoming doubts and following his course to the end, others becoming resigned to a permanent loss of faith, with a melancholy sense that something important has departed from their lives. Yet what exactly are these icy blasts that turn doubters back from the secular life? We have seen how secular humanism can allow value judgments to be more than matters of whimsical preference, and how it can defend the potential meaningfulness of human lives. It fares no worse than refined religion in confronting the prospect of our own death and the certainty that we shall not be reunited with those we have loved and lost: any greater consolation religion provides in the face of death depends on embracing fiction as fact. Yet, even though value, meaning, and mortality are the most obvious sources for articulating what has been lost, a sense that something essential has vanished lingers, even when the explicit challenges have been addressed.

Unsatisfied by answers to precise questions, Levin and his descendants turn to metaphor.

So, for example, in a rightly influential book, Charles Taylor charges that secular life is "flattened," that it has lost a dimension. Secular conceptions treat the world as a plane, constituted by physical, organic, and human interactions, which jointly generate the secular versions of values and meaning: secular lives are those of flatlanders. Religious perspectives add something orthogonal to the plane, an axis that links us to the transcendent, giving depth to our lives. William James brings out the same structural idea with a different metaphor. The secular are like the tone-deaf, unable to apprehend the value of a symphony. In consequence, their lives are deprived of "insight into depths of truth unplumbed by the discursive intellect."

Soft atheism allows for the possibility, even embraces the probability, that there is more to reality than the picture supported by the evidence now available includes. Future inquiry is likely to overturn some presently well grounded conceptions and to enlarge our vision—it might even show that the extra "dimension" exists and that particular types of processes link us to a distinct, "transcendent," realm. Although the scenario is possible, it is highly unlikely, given the current state of knowledge, and there is every reason to think all of the clashing doctrines the world's religions have proposed about the transcendent are thoroughly false. Refined faith in an unknowable transcendent is legitimate, but offers no consolation to those who feel the chill of secularism. People with a keen sense of loss may well begin with a leap of faith to an abstract transcendent, only to fall back into the fictions of unrefined religion—that is why boundary drawing is so important. Moreover, even at its purest, refined religion can easily be diverted into abstractions that obscure the human realities and the human problems. When the songs are sung by sirens, it is better to be tone-deaf.

Leaving the discussion with so blunt a dismissal is, however, unsatisfactory. Religious people and those who regret their loss of faith resist being told that they are guilty of wishful thinking and guesswork. When something important is lost by abandoning belief and when it is known that the evidence is incomplete, continued faith is entirely reasonable. Secularists naturally want to know just what their interlocutors see themselves as standing to lose. When they are informed that no literal specification can be given, that secular lives are "flattened," or are unable to resonate with the music of the eternal, they are often tempted to close the conversation and walk away. I want to resist that temptation.

My strategy throughout this book has been to explore the sense of loss religious people foresee in the transition to a secular perspective. The usual suspects have already been rounded up and dealt with: we've considered the alleged impossibility of a secular source of values, the supposed meaninglessness of finite lives, and the charge of secularist inability to cope with the problems posed by death. What remain are less definite concerns. In attempting to confront them, I may only expose (once again?) my secularist deafness. Yet even if my efforts are inadequate they may serve to prompt those who share the religious sensibility to provide a more forthright elaboration.

Either of two distinct visions of human life can inspire these indefinite concerns. One of these, the one so far emphasized, adopts a relatively positive view of the secular human condition: the religious life further enhances what might be judged an already acceptable state. It promises enrichment and depth. The rival perspective supposes the human predicament in the absence of religion to be deeply problematic: secular humanism ignores the darkness in human nature. Secularists can only provide a diluted brew, suited perhaps to the lives of closeted intellectuals—they fortify those who must do battle, with their own demons and with the roughness of life, by offering cups of weak tea. Religion is needed to rescue human life from darkness and depravity.

Depth and depravity are obverse images of the envisaged loss. I shall start with depth.

II

The most obvious way of pointing to the added depth a religious perspective can bring is to recall the power of momentary experiences in which people suddenly feel a surge of joy, uniting them with nature and affirming for them the beauty, order, and value of the universe. Reports of religious experiences provide large numbers of examples, often occurring to people at a particular stage of life (late adolescence), at a particular time of year (spring), at particular times of day (early morning or evening), in a particular setting (familiar countryside under unusually beautiful light). Allegedly such experiences indicate something important about the religious sensibility, showing (as Charles Taylor puts it) that "somewhere, in some activity and condition, lies a fullness, a richness; that is, in that place (activity or condition), life is fuller, richer, deeper, more worthwhile, more admirable, more what it should be." Recollections of the experiences permeate the subsequent career of the subject, transforming her life into something more profound. Secular existence lacks this depth, this sense of fullness.

People without commitments to traditional forms of religion often have experiences with many similar features. Famous occurrences seem to have taken place above Tintern Abbey or in prospect of Mont Blanc, and many thoroughly irreligious people could add instances from their own lives. They would report the joy, the unity, even the affirmation of particular values, of a sense that this is how life should be. The principal difference between the religious reports and those secularists would offer consists in the former instance of a felt connection to "something beyond," often described by the believer in the categories of the tradition to which he adheres.

In deciding whether a religious perspective enhances the value of these experiences—"epiphanies," I shall call them—two distinct questions arise. The first concerns the momentary character of the epiphany: does the understanding of it as an emanation from the transcendent make what is felt, here and now, richer, fuller, and deeper? The second focuses on the pervasive effects of the vision: does perceived connection to the transcendent confer a power to transform the life in which the epiphany is a passing moment? Although I take the heart of the religious claim to be its answer to the second question, its thought that human *lives* receive depth from religious conviction, both issues deserve consideration.

Taylor's formulation might be read as claiming for the religious life a kind of joy that secular existence cannot deliver, or, even more radically: secular experience always falls short of joy, settling for mere pleasure. The account of the meaningful life in the previous chapter was sober, even Puritanical; it said nothing about pleasure, let alone joy. In this it followed tradition. From the ancient world on, discussions of the valuable life have typically—and with good reason—resisted hedonism, the thesis that life is worthwhile insofar as it is filled with pleasures and with the absence of pain. Meaningful lives surely require more than permanent infusions of Soma or uninterrupted residence in the Orgasmatron. To deny the sufficiency of pleasure (and the absence of pain) is not, however, to contend that enjoyment is irrelevant to the worthwhile life. A dour human existence, in which worthy goals were set, pursued with perseverance, and often achieved, without any sense of happy fulfillment or exhilaration, would be lacking an important dimension.

People often regret—sometimes bitterly—their pursuit of pleasures that interfere with attainment of their aims. Nevertheless, the everyday pleasures that neither promote nor detract from fulfillment of central desires are not to be despised—they are often adornments of a worthwhile life. Moreover, some everyday pleasures are interwoven with the projects of a life's theme, and especially with respect to these, it is possible for secular lives to exemplify the qualities Taylor reserves for the religious epiphany. Uplift and joy are not banished from the secular life.

Secular joy is most intense, perhaps, when pleasure is allied to the sense of one life touching another, in the fulfilling experiences of a happy marriage, in the communion of friendship, in delight at the happiness of a child. Joy can be even more profound in appreciating the happiness felt by a loved one whose own joy comes from an act of giving. A grandfather observes the instant transformation of his son into a father, as he holds his own infant son in his arms, and the observation resonates with all the memories of a loving relationship spanning three decades. It is hard for me to believe that the depth, complexity, and richness of this experience is, in any way, lacking.

Secular and religious people may well take their joy in different places. The strictly celibate monk will not share the joy of the secular grandparent, nor will the latter feel the uplift of the monk's devotions. Moments of joy are likely to be distributed differently across secular and religious lives. For some people, aesthetic pleasure, whether in the presence of nature or in the experience of works of art, may be an important part of their lives—although even here there is frequently an impulse to share, to bring others into contact with the source of uplift. Once secular joy is understood as a reality, excluding it from epiphanies seems unwarranted. Given the profundity of the poems they wrote, it would be dubious speculative psychology to suppose that Shelley beholding Mont Blanc or Wordsworth above Tintern Abbey (or in the thick of the French Revolution) could enjoy only experiences that were pallid counterparts of the ones available to the religious believer.

Turn now to the second question, the more important issue of the pervasive role of epiphanies in human lives. From William James on, sophisticated students of religious experience have recognized that there are many alternative hypotheses as to why epiphanies come about when they do. Religious people favor one hypothesis: epiphanies are communications from a transcendent realm normally hidden from us. There's no reason to prefer that hypothesis to any of a myriad others, hypotheses that would invoke combinations of physical, physiological, and psychological causes, the vast majority of which we don't currently know how to pursue or even adequately to conceptualize. Epiphanies happen. But, like many other kinds of human experiences, much remains to be discovered about their nature and their causes.

Does the religious commitment to interpreting epiphanies as interactions with the transcendent confer on them a special status, making them more likely to work a permanent transformation? Perhaps this is Taylor's position—it is surely one favored by many religious thinkers. A verse of George Herbert's expresses the idea with simple eloquence: seeing God in all things transforms existence.

A servant with this clause
Makes drudgery divine;

Who sweeps a room as for Thy laws
Makes that and th' action fine.

When epiphanies are credited with a connection to the transcendent, the sense of added dignity pervades the life that follows.

Yet that is to adopt a controversial psychological hypothesis. A secular alternative would take the enduring power of some epiphanies to transform people's subsequent lives to stem from the qualities of the experience itself, not from speculations about its causes, but from the sense of uplift and unity, from the conviction of an important insight into how things should be. Those who succeed in fixing the moment in memory, and who can later turn their recollections toward it, reap the pervasive benefits it supplies, whether or not they are religious or secular, whatever beliefs they have about its causes.

Eighty years ago, in *A Common Faith* (his Terry Lectures), John Dewey saw the essential point:

> It is the claim of religions that they effect this generic and enduring change in attitude. I should like to turn the statement around and say that whenever this change takes place there is a definitely religious attitude. It is not *a* religion that brings it about, but when it occurs, from whatever cause and by whatever means, there is a religious outlook and function.

As Dewey confessed elsewhere in his lectures, his encompassing use of religious vocabulary could be seen as stretching concepts too far. Like many of Dewey's secular readers, I prefer to label the crucial episodes more neutrally—hence my term 'epiphanies'—distinguishing religious and secular perspectives on them according to the hypotheses offered about their causes. Dewey was right, however, to recognize that epiphanies are valuable, that they can transform the lives of those who have them, and he was insightful to insist that their power to do so is independent of the subjects' hypotheses about their causes. The crucial factor in the enduring power of epiphanies lies in a strong conviction of their significance, a significance appreciable by recognizing their connection with values to which subjects are already committed.

As things actually stand, the motive force felt by people whose epiphanies are framed in religious terms may be greater than that impinging on their secular counterparts. That conjecture might be true as a side consequence of a point recognized in the previous chapter: the most prominent world religions have lavished a great deal of time on refining their rites and teachings. If they have adapted to satisfy human psychological and social needs, they may supply environments for the believer in which the transformative capacities of epiphanies are enhanced. Yet attraction to any such conjecture or any putative explanation of it ought to be tempered by recognition that the effects of epiphanies are often fleeting, even for those who think of them as manifestations of the transcendent. A writer who made skilful use of epiphanies in charting the development of his protagonist offers a telling example. Stephen Dedalus, having sought and received absolution for his sexual transgressions, returns to the family kitchen, and is struck by a vision of everyday beauty. Confession and atonement inspire an epiphany in which familiar things are seen anew:

> On the dresser was a plate of sausages and white puddings and on the shelf there were eggs. They would be for the breakfast in the morning after the communion in the college chapel. White pudding and eggs and sausages and cups of

tea. How simple and beautiful was life after all. And life lay all before him.

Stephen responds by dedicating himself to a rigorous schedule of rituals and devotions that drain his experience of its vitality. Although he is remarkable for the frequency of his epiphanies, their power to achieve a stable effect on his life is limited. The significance, so vivid in the moment, fades—and even the machinery of religion itself contributes to eroding the effects of his epiphany.

There should be no automatic presumption that religious believers are especially predisposed to having their lives transformed for the better. Indeed, once it is appreciated that the central issue concerns the enduring positive effects of a type of experience available to religious and secular subjects alike, it should be clear that a large number of empirical questions are in danger of being begged. Do epiphanies typically have long-term positive effects? Do they occur more frequently in the lives of religious people than in those of the secular? If so, is that a pattern that would inevitably disappear in different, thoroughly secular cultural environments? Are the consequences for believers likely to be more enduring and more positive than those for unbelievers? What factors make it more probable that epiphanies will result in pervasive positive transformations? Even if such factors are presently found more frequently in the lives of the religious, would it be possible to make those factors commonplace in completely secular societies?

These questions are not easy to address. The lot of a sober social scientist who tried to investigate them systematically would not be an entirely happy one. Taylor, like William James before him, is right to point to the valuable roles epiphanies sometimes play in human lives. Yet the supposition that the positive effects are stronger, or even only available, under the aegis of religious belief—that the lives of the nonreligious are somehow "flattened"—is simply conjecture. How the good consequences can be achieved more frequently, contributing to a more lasting transformation, is a matter for intricate inquiry. We can only experiment.

III

A different, but related, thought is that the lives of the religious are pervaded by a confidence secular humanists cannot enjoy. At its best, religion is refined, eschewing specific readings of the traditional stories in favor of a commitment to important values and ideals, which it regards as linked to the transcendent. The thought can be developed in either of two ways. According to the weaker version, the transcendent connection underwrites a sense that the realization of those ideals and values is possible. The stronger claims that, with appropriate human effort, success is assured: in the words T. S. Eliot adapted from Julian of Norwich, "All shall be well, and all manner of thing shall be well." A beautiful lyric of Rilke's unfolds the promise further: it envisages the fall of the autumn leaves as a sign of universal decay and falling, seen also in the fall of the hands of the aged, the fall of the earth and of the physical universe—and yet perceives, under all, a sustaining pair of hands in which the fate of everything is secure.

Modest refined religion can endorse Rilke's powerful metaphor, but only as metaphor. To go further, to think of existent hands and of an existent deity to whom they belong would contaminate the refinement of the religious perspective. Religious believers who take that further step, perhaps affirming a fatherly creator, whose perfect goodness combines with omnipotence and omniscience, are committed to a strong providentialism. Not only are they vulnerable to the arguments against substantive doctrine presented in Chapter 1. Their confidence must also engage a dialectic that has motivated atheism from Epicurus to Hume to Dostoyevsky's Ivan Karamazov and beyond.

What basis for hope and confidence does refined religion supply? Committed to the unknowability of the transcendent, it accepts the transcendent on the basis of faith, coupled with hope that the sustaining hands are an apt metaphor, and that, in consequence, all shall be well. The believer is a cousin of James's solitary mountaineer, willing himself into belief that he can make the difficult leap. Appreciating the kinship undercuts any thought of a confidence secularists cannot match. Irreligious climbers sometimes save their lives by working themselves into a state of conviction that an abyss can be crossed in a single bound. More significantly, people have sometimes achieved great goals by persuading themselves, against all odds, that they would succeed—nations have won their freedom and human rights have been extended out of unjustified confidence that the cause would triumph. Unless the sustaining hands are treated as articles of known doctrine—and the purity of refined religion thereby compromised—the hopes of refined believers and of secularists are on a par.

In the face of serious human problems, those posed by attempts to realize the egalitarian ideal, for example, the usefulness of hope should not be underestimated. If the religious commitment is to the weaker version of providentialism, to the *possibility* of realizing values, a secular perspective again allows a corresponding hope and confidence, attained by a less dubious and circuitous route. Responding to the aspirations of all, providing for every human being the preconditions of a meaningful life, might require refiguring contemporary economic institutions and committing ourselves to global sociopolitical reform, but it would be premature to dismiss the goal as unattainable and consequently to abandon hope. If skeptics challenge the ideal, arguing that it is unrealizable, hope should be refined through addressing the challenges explicitly. Perhaps the arguments can be refuted, and confidence thereby buttressed. Or perhaps it is necessary to reformulate previous aims in the light of the evidence, rather than continuing to insist on a quixotic venture. Readjustment *benefits* from not being bound by some supposed transcendent guarantee. Better to follow the evidence, to hope when skeptical arguments can be neutralized, and to modify goals when the objections reveal their power.

Commitment to a minimal providentialism does no harm, except when it interferes with the reasonable revision of ethical ideals. The stronger providentialist doctrine that envisages guaranteed success ("All shall be well") is more dangerous, in its tendencies to induce quietism. If the depth of the religious life stems from confident serenity engendered by faith in the presence of protective hands, it is perhaps better to be gripped by the "shallower" attitude that clearly sees the horror of some human situations, that lacks the reassurance of some grander scheme into which everything fits. Better to be dedicated to saving *these people* who suffer *here* and *now*. Failures to rescue them cannot—*should not*—be viewed from the perspective of some allegedly grander ethical order in which what is most valuable is inevitably victorious. Even though it is easy to understand how those who suffer can find solace in comforting illusions, their prospects are better if people who might relieve their plight adopt a more clear-eyed view. For the losses of the afflicted are real. Each life that goes badly is a cause for mourning, and should be a stimulus to renewed human effort, rather than an occasion to take confidence from the thought of an "ultimate compensation." For those who might help, faith in future redemption is an irresponsible illusion.

My complaint about the dangers of strong providentialism mirrors one often directed toward secular humanism, the charge that when ethical precepts are separated from a grounding in the transcendent their claims are less exacting: ethical life is allegedly more "strenuous" when it is embedded in religion. James declares that, for those who believe "in a merely human world without a God, the appeal to our moral energy falls short of its maximal stimulating power." A secular worldview cannot substitute the thought of realizing ideals through benefiting future generations, because, James contends, this thought lacks "the infinite perspective." He concludes by connecting his claims with the greater depth of the religious life:

> The capacity of the strenuous mood lies so deep down among our natural human possibilities that even if there were no metaphysical or traditional grounds for believing in a God, men would postulate one simply as a pretext for living hard, and getting out of the game of existence its keenest possibilities of zest.

It is a curious fact about the metaphor of depth that some thinkers locate the fullness of the religious life in the confidence, hope, and serenity faith affords, while others, like James, take it to consist in the excitement of the "strenuous mood." Does secular humanism evade one form of objection only to fall victim to its mirror image?

I'll address this question by starting with another: What, exactly, does religious belief add to the force of an ethical imperative? An obvious answer, although not the one James offers, is that religions strengthen ethical motivations by presenting the prospect of eternal rewards and of eternal punishment. Given the popularity of the transcendent policeman as a character in the ethnographic record, the reinforcement of ethical motivation by religion is a common strategy—and the punishments the policeman will inflict are often lavishly described with graphic details. But securing compliance through terror achieves only a primitive form of ethical life, one refined when different emotions and attitudes are recruited to guide people toward better conduct. Moreover, when ethical transgressions are dramatically linked to intense eternal punishment, as in Christian and Muslim conceptions of an afterlife of infinite suffering, questions of the justice of the arrangements become unavoidable. How could *finite* lives, no matter how blotted by appalling crimes, ever deserve *eternal* torment (especially when it is described in the graphic terms of the pamphlets Joyce drew on as sources for the sermons that terrified Stephen Dedalus)? How could people whose major fault lay in failure to believe, under conditions in which the deity seems to take a willful delight in not sending clear signals, be justly condemned to so horrific a fate? To take the language of descriptions of Hell as metaphor probably detracts from the motivating force, but, so long as the metaphors are apt, similar concerns about justice must arise. If the transcendent is to be identified with the source of ethical values, it must be seen as the ground of justice—even, as Dante claimed, of love. Consequently, Christian and Muslim doctrines of the afterlife, with their division of the redeemed from the permanently damned, cannot be seen as anything other than bizarre fictions. If divine sanctions are to be just, they must answer to the standards of mundane justice, abandoning grotesque disproportion between crime and punishment. Transcendent retribution would then be no more "strenuous" than its secular counterpart.

James's own account improves on gothic fantasy. Religious reinforcement of ethical imperatives derives from seeing actions as directed toward ends, whose significance lies in their having "the note of infinitude." But there is less to this resounding rhetoric than meets the eye or ear. Supposedly, the ethical acts of the religious believer are directed by a sense of contributing to the eternal order; humanists strive only to better the condition of future people, a "remote posterity" whom they do not love "keenly enough." Here James falls into the familiar trap of taking ethics to be concerned with identifying a fixed and final system, whose precepts are to be exemplified in human conduct, in thinking of "progress to" rather than of "progress from." The utopian condition of future human life has no great motivating force—and, by virtue of the resounding language used to describe it, the eternal cosmic order should win any advertising campaign. The real spur to ethical action and to ethical improvement, however, lies in recognition of the urgency of human problems. Ethical life, under a secular perspective, is strenuous not because we care about achieving some ideal future human state— that should move us as little or as much as the prospect of realizing some large, equally remote cosmic order—but because the lives of actual people are so easily blighted, distorted, truncated, deprived of happiness, and shorn of meaning. Recognizing these aspects of our world gives impetus enough to the ethical life.

James begins his investigation of ethics by taking its origins to lie in responses to demands made by others, and, after his detour through the contrast between "finite" and "infinite" ideals, he concludes with a different argument in favor of the depth of the religious perspective. He sees an important distinction between the attitude an ethical agent would feel toward "concrete evils," when the only existent beings are "finite demanders," and the joy felt in facing tragedy "for an infinite demander's sake." So, he maintains, energy, endurance, and courage are "set free in those who have religious faith."

Although this second defense of the strenuousness of the religiously embedded ethical life improves on the first by focusing attention on the source of the ethical project—aspirations and failures in adequate response to them—it is vitiated by a crucial ambiguity. Those who issue demands, who suffer or who are in want, might be finite or infinite in virtue of the scale of their needs; alternatively, their lives and capacities might count as finite or infinite. Arguably, the magnitude of the suffering or want should affect the intensity of the efforts to remedy it, so that a being infinitely lacking—if any such being is conceivable—should inspire the largest and strongest dedication of energy, endurance, and courage to respond to its desperate plight. Deities, however, are not usually taken to be like that. They are infinite in different senses, incomparably great rather than infinitely deficient. Whatever demands they make do not stem from a lack more profound than human suffering. The criterion for the intensity of demand thus shifts, from the ethically defensible thought that the most urgent needs and largest forms of suffering should be met with the greatest dedication, to the idea that any scale of demand made by a being of sufficiently grand attributes should be honored. According to this new standard, people who participated in historical atrocities, "simply following the orders" of their powerful commanders, would be vindicated. When James's ambiguity is exposed, the religious embedding should be seen as a hideous distortion of the properly strenuous—humanist—ethical life.

A last version of the complaint appears to arise with particular force against the account of the ethical project defended in Chapter 2. For that account views human beings as the collective source of values—our negotiations with one another generate them—so that ethical precepts are inventions, not discoveries of any independent, possibly transcendent, order. Is it possible to take seriously rules we have fashioned? From early in their lives, people distinguish between conventions and ethical imperatives, crediting the latter with extra stringency—even young children know that breaking the rules of a game doesn't justify hitting the rule-breaker. When ethics is viewed as a purely human project, do its precepts lose the overriding importance an external source, perhaps a transcendent source, would confer upon them?

Part of the answer lies in recognizing that the ethical project has generated distinctions among types of norms. What began as an undifferentiated collection of rules for life together was broken up into categories, as our ancestors came to understand how precepts could conflict. Their decisions about priority have engendered important distinctions, including in most cultural traditions the conception of ethical imperatives as dominating others. Techniques of socialization, interacting perhaps with evolved propensities to be disturbed by the expressed suffering of others, emphasize those distinctions. Well-brought-up children quickly learn the difference between lapsing from the rules of a game of make-believe and attacking another player.

So much is only part of the answer, however. For even though human decisions may legislate that some conventions take priority over others, my account of the ethical project seems to make all the imperatives conventional. Some games whose rules we devise may be stipulated as more fundamental than others, but, in the end, they are all games of our own making. Yet that is a misleading way to formulate the challenge. The standards and precepts that emerge in the ethical project are not matters of individual decision, nor are they made arbitrarily. Ethics is a collective venture, undertaken to address the problems constitutive of the human predicament. Chapter 2 replaced the external standard imposed by some remote transcendent realm, not with the freedom to make arbitrary conventions as anyone pleases, but with a collective reaction to the difficulties unfolding from our limited responsiveness to others. Secular Kantians attempt to bring an objective moral order close to home, contrasting the "starry heavens above" with the "moral law within," and identifying practical reason as the source of ethical truth. I have attempted a similar transference from some dim and remote ground of ethical objectivity to a fundamental feature of the human condition—our need to live with others, and our evolved incapacity for doing that without continual strife. Reflection on ethics as a common human project sparked by that fundamental feature, a project that has made us the beings we are, should make life committed to continuing that project strenuous enough.

IV

I have been focusing on religious life as a positive enhancement of a secular form of existence, a mode of living seen as tolerable but lacking depths that human experience might plumb. Turn now to the different thought that religion corrects intolerable deficiencies. Religious commitment is needed, not to add more "zest" to life—as if religion were optional seasoning—but to rescue humanity from the darkness of human nature, from the depravity to which we are all prone.

You may think that, like Dewey's plea in *A Common Faith*, my defense of secularism has been pervaded by a naive optimism. It has presupposed a picture of the human subject, admittedly limited in its capacities for responding to others, but able, nonetheless, to improve, to come to appreciate the claims of fellow beings, to reflect, to arrive at reasonable conclusions, and, in light of those conclusions, to overcome prior indifference. Human beings have been conceived as superior versions of Hobbesian egoists, equipped with a little other-directedness that makes life together possible and with a lot of talent for calm reflection. Out of this conception grow hopes for ethical progress, for meaningful lives, and for secular replacements for the valuable ends served by religious communities at their best.

But what if we were worse than that? Reasonable people, mostly but not entirely selfish, might be capable of the lives my secular humanism commends, but—a pessimistic voice whispers—they would be ludicrous fantasies for *real* human beings: beings with unsteady, easily subverted propensities for reasoning and reflection, with tendencies sometimes to desire, intensely desire, ends that would wreck the aspirations they form "in the cool hour," perhaps even to harbor those self-destructive urges because of deep resentment and hatred of others, aiming through their self-lacerating acts to heap greater suffering on their detested targets. Real people need the discipline of religion, not to add "zest," but in order to tame their demons and make possible some minimal value for their lives.

Bleak thoughts about human depravity might arise from remembering the extent of cruelty in recorded history, the occasions on which, under the sway of religion and secular regimes alike, people have done appalling things to one another. Pessimists suppose this dark record testifies to enduring sources of human depravity, unable to be completely disciplined by any social environments we know how to devise. Champions of religion contend that the best forms of discipline, able to check the destructive impulses but not to eradicate them, require a religious framework. The pervasiveness of religion across human cultures testifies to the need for restraint, not in the shallow form of the transcendent policeman, but in a vivid consciousness of the sinful human condition. No secular surrogates are available. Those who attempt to throw off religious restraint should expect to forfeit the qualities of human life they value most.

The convictions underlying pessimism of this sort do not stem from rigorously grounded forms of psychological understanding or from scientific evidence about the inevitable eruption of dark tendencies under a wide range of social environments. Perhaps someday careful inquiry will establish conclusions supporting a somber vision of our nature, but, for the moment, those who endorse that vision do so on a different basis. Some may be convinced by the writings of philosophers, moved perhaps by Schopenhauer's conception of a disruptive will as the fundamental reality. More likely is the influence of religious traditions, doctrines of original sin transferred into a more abstract perspective. The chief sources of pessimism are, I conjecture, interpretations of human history and of personal experience in light of writings taken to provide profound analyses. People discern the destructive tendencies manifest in the historical record in their own lives and thoughts, mercifully on a far smaller scale. Turning to the greatest works of literature, they come to perceive the tendencies exposed as indelibly inscribed in human nature.

Secular humanists often dismiss such dyspeptic visions, but I want to conclude this book by taking them seriously. Like Dewey, I suppose works of literature have historically played an important role in fostering human appreciation of what is valuable and in probing the conditions of its realization. So I end with a brief look at two masterpieces challenging the picture of the human subject figuring tacitly in many of my proposals.

V

First, I consider a vision of life in a world whose gods are absent or indifferent. One way to read *King Lear* sees it as demolishing the optimistic conception that the limits of our mutual responsiveness can be overcome, that precepts can be negotiated "in the cool hour" and a stable social order achieved. The play begins from the appearance of order, opening with an attempt to institute a contract to preserve that order beyond the death of the figure who has apparently sustained it by means of his immense authority (the quality Kent discerns in his countenance). Lear's endeavor to prevent "future strifes" is grounded in distrust of the efficacy of positive emotions— what he demands is not love but a performance, the profession of love. Because the performance is public, supposedly carried out and witnessed by rational, if self-centered, agents, it will be enforced, even after the powerful Lear has left the scene. The ceremony goes awry, of course, already a signal that at least one of Lear's daughters is no Hobbesian egoist.

On this reading, the play's shattering impact comes from its presentation of wanton destructiveness as deeply ingrained in human nature: indeed, so deeply and powerfully that it subverts our tendencies to limited responsiveness or rational selfishness. Violent impulses in the human will simply cannot be tamed by contracts and laws and rules, or by any mechanisms with which those can be reinforced. Stable society can be preserved, for limited periods, through the exercise of authority, possibly benign, more likely itself brutal. Lear himself will eventually come to view what is called "justice" as the expression of arbitrary power and of dark desires—at a moment when he is capriciously and sadistically tormenting the blind Gloucester. Sooner or later, though, whatever order is sustained by these ugly mechanisms must collapse. Rulers or ruling institutions age, and the world is returned not to the Hobbesian state of nature (for there is none) but to the naked manifestation of the dark, disruptive tendencies, to the open expression of something akin to Schopenhauer's destructive "Will."

Lear's plan fails because he mistakes the human condition. So too does Cornwall. In an ironic echo of Lear's miscalculation, Cornwall appraises Edmund.

Natures of such deep trust we shall much need
You we first seize on.

The judgment has nothing to do with Edmund's powers of deception or Cornwall's gullibility. Cornwall recognizes Edmund's ambition, classifies him as a Machiavellian calculator—and with such people one can deal, since it is simply a matter of finding the right incentives. Yet, with one exception, the mild Albany, none of the inhabitants of this world follow the counsels of prudence. How far the voice of reason may go is made evident in Goneril's dismissive response to her husband's advice "not to mar what's well." So too, at the end of the play, Albany judiciously withdraws from the work of finding a way to go on: "reasonable men" are not suited to sustain a world like this.

Destruction and self-destruction well up everywhere. Goneril and Regan agree in wanting to "disquantity" Lear's train, to reduce the number of his followers from the hundred the initial contract had assigned him. They cannot resist a gratuitous expansion of their project, entering into a competition to refuse their father's requests to the utmost limit. Edmund, aware from his first words to his last of his own nature, wants not only advancement but also to inflict pain and misery on his father and his brother. Yet he cannot resist a risky dalliance. Machiavelli would surely recommend tying his fortunes to the widowed Regan, or committing himself to the project of widowing Goneril, but Edmund relishes a situation in which he can remain undecided between two options, his vanity enjoying the rivalry between the jealous sisters.

The power of destructive urges, wishes that reach so far beyond what is instrumental in achieving egoistic goals that they are committed to harming others even at cost to attaining selfish ends, is most fully developed in the blinding of Gloucester. Assuming Cornwall and Regan are sincere in supposing Gloucester to have knowledge of a French invasion, there are many ways to deal with him. Regan first proposes to hang the old man at once; it is her sister who anticipates the blinding that will eventually occur. Before Cornwall has taken command of the situation, Regan appears to be satisfied with punishment rather than interrogation. Later, after Gloucester is bound, the torture begins methodically—pulling some facial hair might warm the old man up for confession. But the interrogators enjoy themselves too much, launching questions pell-mell until Gloucester's resistance spurs them to abandon questioning entirely in favor of the wanton infliction of pain. Cornwall and Regan cannot contain their revels, provoking, as they might have anticipated, even loyal followers to protest. The *questioning* ends—transmutes itself into providing Gloucester with information about Edmund's role, another turn of the sadistic screw—and, without trying to learn anything further, Regan commands that the old man be thrust out. Nothing has been discovered—and yet Cornwall and Regan are exultant, their pleasure marred only by the wound the "villein" has inflicted.

Nor can we find consolation in the thought that stable order is undermined because, as well as incomplete altruists, the world contains a few individuals who can be moved by a destructive force beyond rational egoism. The same tendencies appear in Lear himself: in the banishment of Cordelia and Kent, in his furious decision to go out into the storm, in the sadistic taunting of Gloucester (whose identity and condition he recognizes), and in his "delicate stratagem" for dealing with his sons-in-law (". . . kill, kill, kill, kill, kill, kill!"). Even in Kent and Cordelia, love, devotion, and loyalty must overcome irrational destructive urges. Kent's catalogue of insults to Oswald goes beyond expressing dedication to Lear's cause—its gratuitous gibes find pleasure in the outpouring of hatred and contempt, even if the consequence is a contest his master must lose. Cordelia likewise assumes an unnecessary—and provocative—plainness in formulating her contractual obligations to her father, most evidently in reminding him that he must share her love with her future husband. Kent and Cordelia personify a rare and admirable responsiveness to others—yet their altruism has limits, bounds not charted by their selfish desires (neither evinces any), but by immoderate wishes to shatter whatever threatens the things they love.

Nor can these destructive urges be tamed by recognizing them and imposing a firm discipline. Edgar is as self-aware as his brother. He reacts to the threat of disorder, visible in the world without and perceived in the psyche within, by adopting an extreme stoicism, one in which his own identity is voluntarily abandoned and canceled in the attempt to reduce his desires and aspirations to a level at which even the most cruel world would permit them to be satisfied. Having escaped the hunt, he resolves to take on bestial form, to become the most abject type of humanity—Edgar is erased in "poor Tom." As he learns, even this minimal version of human existence demands too much. At the moment when he congratulates himself on having reduced his hopes, he learns of the savagery inflicted on his father—and the process of self-obliteration must go yet further. Its course is charted by the motto he has already given himself: "Lurk, lurk!"

Stoicism is intensified even after he has heard his father's own confession of renewed love:

> O dear son Edgar,
> The food of thy abused father's wrath,
> Might I but live to see thee in my touch,
> I'd say I had eyes again.

Although it proves hard, Edgar can still "lurk." Not only can he deliver a virtuoso performance in the pantomime of Gloucester's attempted suicide—switching personae mid-scene with aplomb—but he can maintain his strategy to the moments before his father's death. Only when he is armed does he allow Gloucester the chance to "see him" in his touch. Perhaps that does provide a cure for the old man's despair, indeed the only possible cure, a release from the task of enduring, the canceling of bodily existence, a final respite from the tortures of human life.

People who are prey to such dark urges cannot be disciplined by rules and contracts, bound in harmonious interactions, provided with the stable preconditions for meaningful lives. In the play's closing lines, an alternative is strangely placed in the mouth of the stoical Edgar.

> The weight of this sad time we must obey,
> Speak what we feel, not what we ought to say.
> The oldest hath borne most; we that are young
> Shall never see so much, nor live so long.

Speak what we feel? That was never an option—and reasonably so. Lear knew from the beginning that human emotional responses could never sustain the order he intended to preserve. What Edgar has learned is that other strategies are no less inadequate, and that the consequence is the diminishing and truncation of human lives in a world that is "cheerless, dark, and deadly."

Social order can be achieved, for a while, by the exercise of power, almost certainly capricious, and probably unjust, but it cannot survive the decay and death of the contingent figures who wield it. An enduring solution to Lear's problem might be found if authority could be grounded in something beyond the finite, human realm. Lear's world does not allow for that. Appeals to the "clearest gods" go unanswered. If they exist, they are indifferent, if not cruel:

As flies to wanton boys are we to the gods,
They kill us for their sport.

Any deities are made in Cornwall's image.

VI

Not so, however, for my second literary illustration. While Dostoyevsky's *Brothers Karamazov* adopts a similarly bleak vision of the unregenerate human condition, the novel envisages a solution, even redemption, in a version of orthodox Christianity committed to substantive doctrines about the transcendent. The theme is introduced in presenting the career of Ivan, the "clever" brother, author of the most forceful version of the problem of evil ever formulated, and of a "poem," the parable of the Grand Inquisitor, designed to expose the terrible burden inflicted on feeble humanity by the injunction to Christian love. Ivan's initial refusal to accept God, accompanied by a theoretical understanding of human evil and a confidence in his power to discipline his own passions, gives way to a later condition of confusion, guilt, and horror, culminating in his collapse in the courtroom. The reality of evil, not only in the actions of others but within himself, is brought vividly home to him. His confidence in self-restraint is unmasked as naive bravado, inadequate for coping with the abysses of his nature. Reflection on what he has permitted, encouraged, and done becomes unbearable. Ivan's career is naturally read as a warning to secular humanism, as a vivid depiction of the fragility of life without God.

Ivan is closer than he suspects to his father, the "insect" Fyodor, and to his half-brother Dmitri. Ivan takes perverse pleasure in watching his pupil, Smerdyakov, play cruelly with the naive faith of his fellow servant, Grigory. Looking on, the old sensualist Fyodor displays a previously hidden talent for reasoning—the traits of father and son are more mixed than their original introductions suggested.

Similarly, the apparent contrast between cool, perceptive Ivan and thoughtless, impulsive Dmitri is already questioned by Dmitri's early confession of a self-understanding that Ivan will eventually achieve and by which he will be broken. Dmitri explains why his efforts to restrain his depravity fail:

> Because I'm a Karamazov. Because when I fall into the abyss, I go straight into it, head down and heels up, and I'm even pleased that I'm falling in just such a humiliating position, and for me I find it beautiful. And so in that very shame I suddenly begin a hymn.

To be a Karamazov—to be a human being—is to live in self-contradiction, to feel the force of impulses that cannot be reconciled.

Dmitri's psychological life is a "fantastic whirlwind." Blown in directions that change abruptly, he can achieve no coherent course in his dealings with Katya and Grushenka, in his conduct after the fateful visit to his father's house, or in his reactions to his arrest and prosecution. The surges of the inner storm are detailed minutely in the description of his attempt to escape the pursuit of Grigory. Using the brass pestle he has impulsively snatched up, Dmitri hits out in response to the old servant's shouted accusation of parricide. As Grigory falls, Dmitri jumps back into the garden, throws down the pestle, oblivious to the fact that it lands in a conspicuous place, uses his handkerchief to try to stanch the flow of blood from the old man's head, and then, suddenly convinced of the futility of the attempt, climbs over the fence and runs away.

Ivan, too, will come to act like that. On the way to visit Smerdyakov for the third and final time, tormented by the repulsive evil Smerdyakov exhibits and simultaneously exposes in Ivan's own thoughts and life, he is caught by sudden hatred of a stranger encountered by chance, a drunken peasant whom he shoves into the snow. Fully aware that the man will freeze to death, he strides off to his meeting with Smerdyakov. Later, after Smerdyakov's explicit account of the killing of Fyodor has provoked Ivan's decision to tell the whole truth publicly in court, Ivan goes back into the blizzard. With relief, even joy in his decision, he prevents the murder he had almost—quite casually—committed, pulling the peasant out of the snow, arranging and providing "liberally" for his care. Yet joy vanishes as quickly as it came. Back at home, he feels sick, without strength—and experiences a nightmare dialogue with the devil.

How do human lives, Karamazov lives, acquire point and meaning, or even any consistent direction? Part of the brilliance of Dostoyevsky's novel lies in leaving readers in the confusion of the whirlwind. So far as the central plot is concerned, the action simply ceases. Dmitri is unjustly condemned for the murder of his father,

Ivan suffers nervous collapse, the futures of Katya and Grushenka are left entirely indeterminate. The concluding promise of *Crime and Punishment*, Raskolnikov's redemption through hard labor and through Sonia's devotion, finds no analogue in this novel. Instead, the final chapter turns from the inconclusive events in the prison section of the local hospital, where Dmitri is being held and treated, moving to an apparent sideshow, the funeral of the boy Ilyusha.

Choosing that final setting exemplifies both the novel's proposal for coming to terms with Karamazov nature and a sober assessment of what it can accomplish. The possibility of resolving the confusions so evident in Dmitri, of escaping the whirlwind, is presented in the figure of the Elder Zosima. Zosima escaped from a life like Dmitri's by turning to Christ, by embracing a religion founded on love and human service—and his deep bow to Dmitri emphasizes both their kinship and the Elder's recognition of Dmitri's apprehension of his own predicament. Alyosha, the third brother, has been inspired to follow Zosima's path, and the Elder commands him to bring his capacities for love and service to the secular world beyond the monastery walls.

Alyosha is announced as the hero of *Brothers Karamazov*, even as Dostoyevsky apologizes for him (in the narrator's words, "he is by no means a great man"). Seen dispassionately, Alyosha's actions are almost complete failures: he does not prevent the murder, he is unable to forestall the wrongful conviction of Dmitri or to bring the absolution Ivan so desperately needs, his efforts to aid Katya and Grushenka and even Lise lead nowhere. His sole success lies in bringing harmony to the group of schoolboys, in replacing ostracism and contempt with friendship for the dying Ilyusha. Alyosha hopes to instill in the boys capacities for love and forgiveness, fragile and inconstant as they will surely be, urging them at the funeral to remember the example of Ilyusha and to be fortified by it—perhaps his exhortation will prevent the precocious Kolya from following the path Ivan has traveled. Alyosha concludes with a definite promise, avowing substantive Christian doctrine: the dead will rise and there will be reunion in the hereafter.

Alyosha is a novice, an apprentice in the religious life. For someone in training, the problems he is asked to address are usually too big. Success comes only on a small scale, in redirecting the attitudes and the lives of a small number of boys. Yet, Dostoyevsky suggests, small successes are not to be despised. Nor perhaps should we hope for more, even from those who have gone further than Alyosha. Zosima's corpse stinks, the hoped-for miracles do not happen. Karamazov life can only be incompletely corrected, but the work of even partial amendment requires Christian love and Christian hope, founded in faith in Christian doctrine.

From this perspective, both the Grand Inquisitor and the returned Christ whose kiss continues to burn in the Inquisitor's heart are right. Human nature, Karamazov nature, is too weak, confused, irrational, self-destructive, and depraved to allow for meaningful lives and stable order, except under conditions of restraint—yet any such discipline must be founded in and permeated by Christian love. Alyosha's act of plagiarism, the kiss he bestowed on Ivan, failed to redeem his brother. It was, however, the only possibility.

VII

No literary work, however great, can justify accepting illusions as inevitable, and concluding (perhaps regretfully) that human nature is too dark and depraved for us to live even minimally worthwhile lives, unless we subordinate the evidence to blind acceptance of powerful myths. Judgments about the ineradicability of hypothetical human tendencies are premature, whether they issue from speculations in neuroscience or from the conjectures of evolutionary psychology or from works that clearly announce their fictional status. Replacing the structures provided by religious traditions poses practical challenges if all the dimensions of religious community are to be captured—as Chapter 4 acknowledged. Building a fully satisfying, fully secular world will take time, effort, and perhaps luck. But there is no strong evidence for supposing the task to be impossible. No reasons compel us to think worthwhile lives require the sacrifice of factual truth to illusion, or to take the secular program to presuppose an over-rosy vision of human nature. When the proper verdict on pessimism is "not proven," secular humanism should follow the counsel of pragmatism and the direction of the ethical project. Engaging in further "experiments of living," it should seek to adapt the conditions of human life in efforts to proliferate opportunities for all—without continuing to embrace substantive religious doctrines, all of which are almost certainly false, or even to be distracted by faith in an admittedly unknowable transcendent.

. . . and yet. The great works I have all too briefly reviewed can be—should be—profoundly disturbing. They shatter confidence that the foundations on which a secular world is to be built are assured. The possibilities they vividly depict cannot be coolly appraised and eliminated as factually false. The tragic vision does not have to be well supported to be valuable—the provocation of doubt is enough. Doubt needs to be confronted, to be worked through, if the secular world and a secular life are to be crafted and sustained. That may not be a task for everyone, but it is a task for each reflective person—and for a lifetime.

Pragmatic experimentation should be neither blind nor emotionally disengaged nor insufficiently strenuous. Innocent of the potential depth of the problems it attempts to overcome, or unmoved by them, it would only provide tepid possibilities for well-insulated people—for Ivans who never stir beyond the salons of bourgeois St. Petersburg, for Edgars who grow up as only sons under a temporarily stable and benevolent social order. Looking to societies with special features—small, homogeneous, economically buffered—it is tempting to think of religious concerns about what is lost in the transition to a secular world as much ado about very little. "Consider Scandinavia and be encouraged!" declares the secularist, perhaps brandishing the latest data from "happiness research." Much can surely be learned from studying the relatively egalitarian societies of northern Europe, but more can be garnered if the student has faced, and battled with, a vision that sees the supposed achievements as worthless, hollow, or unstable.

Those among Levin's descendants who begin from the thought of human depravity will suppose the pockets of secular happiness are fortunate accidents—Lear's kingdom in its prime, or Ivan's young adulthood. Their counterparts who feel a lack of depth in the secular life will question the "happiness" supposedly achieved. Whether secular success is taken to be genuine but fragile, or simply unreal, the charge, couched in the metaphors this chapter has wrestled with, is that humanity needs a religious cure. Some plaintiffs follow Dostoyevsky and demand the strong medicine of substantive religious doctrine; others advocate refined religion and the continued endorsement of "true myths."

Close scrutiny of the favored metaphors—the "absent dimension," the "unheard music," the "protective hands," the "zest," our "dark urges," our "insect nature"—has replaced vague suggestions of trouble with precise accusations, which can then be rebutted. Yet my rebuttals have been limited. I have argued, in some cases, that secular lives *can* achieve the qualities supposedly available only to the religious, and in others that it has not been shown that they *cannot*. Even if my replies are cogent, it does not follow that many secular lives *will* achieve the valuable features or that a stable, fully satisfying secular world *will* be built—and certainly not that these endeavors will be easy. Deprived of some parts of traditional practice, without language games our forebears used to play, even the best-laid plans of secular architects may be flawed or unrealizable. A secular world might drift into comfortable mediocrity, joy giving way to mere pleasure, baser impulses eventually escaping any restraint. The religious diagnosticians see their traditional doctrines or rites or myths as bulwarks against such possible futures—and that assessment is not refuted by contending that the protection is not strictly necessary, or, even more ineptly, by maintaining that we do not know it to be necessary.

A blunt exhortation to secular experiments will not do. For experiments are sometimes dangerous, and social experiments especially so. Yet I hope my discussions have assembled resources for a last answer to the religious challenge. Modest refined religion embraces a favored collection of "true myths," understood as delivering insights that sustain the refined believer in achieving a more worthwhile life. Cosmopolitan versions propose to draw on the many religious traditions of the world in the quest for human self-understanding (Lessing's Enlightenment drama, *Nathan der Weise*, points the way). My further step is to take the supposedly privileged scriptures to be superseded: they should give way to a more inclusive collection of resources, some of them supplied by the natural and social sciences, but many, probably most, derived from the great artistic achievements, including the great literature, of our species. Insofar as the religious stories figure in this eclectic corpus, they do so *explicitly* as works of fiction. The idea of the religious life, permeated by the doctrines, lore, and rites of a particular tradition, gives way to a different vision: secular life, at its keenest, undertakes a passionate engagement with what it is to be human. Resources for that engagement are found in the corpus I have envisaged.

Chapter 2 argued that the ethical project is complicated by the existence of functional conflict, and offered the example of two clashing ideals: one emphasizes the importance of equality, its rival the proliferation of possibilities for human lives. In responding to this conflict, I proposed that the problem of limited responsiveness remains central for us. Yet that responsiveness is properly developed with a commitment to spreading the opportunities for human life at its richest, and indeed to enlarging the menu of human possibilities. The tug of conflicting ideals should be acknowledged.

Secular egalitarians are easily pulled in one direction. Moved by the degradation of many human lives in the nascent stages of the industrial revolution, Bentham urged attention to aggregate human happiness, conceived as pleasure and the absence of pain (indeed, he went further, focusing on pleasure and pain in *every* creature that can feel them). The contemporary world is full enough of misery and want and suffering to inspire a counterpart of Bentham's demand for equality—each is to count for one, and none for more than one, in the computation of total utility—a call for economic and social arrangements that enable all people to live comfortably, or at least with a modicum of pleasure. Yet it is well to be mindful of the preference expressed by a philosopher partially sympathetic to Bentham. Mill famously declared that a dissatisfied Socrates is better than a contented pig. His emphasis on human worth and dignity gave a secular twist to the religious dictum that we do not live by bread alone.

Committed egalitarians frequently—and correctly—feel the urgency of their task. Faced with the appalling injustices of the worldwide distribution of material goods, and hence of resources and of human possibilities, they are often impatient with the attention given to refined analyses of the human condition. When people are starving, when vast segments of the world's population are ravaged by disease and vulnerable to violence, when children have no serious possibilities for education, why should anyone bother with Camus' sense of human futility or Nietzsche's celebrations of "free spirits," with Proust's explorations of the heart's intermissions or Henry James's probing of human relationships? What relevance is there even in Shakespeare or Dostoyevsky? Profoundly important work waits to be done—*now*—in remedying or ameliorating the plight of millions, even billions.

. . . and yet. Without serious, even passionate, engagement with what great thinkers and writers have explored in the human condition, the secular life is diminished. It may provide security and bodily health, water, bread and even circuses, but the egalitarianism of Chapter 2 sees all these as bases for something further and more significant: the opportunity for a worthwhile life. An unreflective secular perspective can assume that human beings are good enough, reasonable enough, to serve as citizens in an orderly and rewarding secular republic—just as the believer may have faith that "All shall be well, and all manner of thing shall be well." But behind that should stand a division of labor, in which some of the secular citizens probe more deeply. A more profound worth for *all* comes if *some* engage with rival visions, shattering as they often are, working through them to an inevitably provisional resolution. In the end, we need Camus as well as Fanon and Gandhi, Proust as well as Marx and Orwell, Shakespeare and Dostoyevsky as well as Darwin and Einstein, Tonio Kröger as well as Hans Hansen and Ingeborg Holm.

Crafting a fully secular world must be a pragmatic enterprise. But the crafting of that world, and of individual lives within it, should be self-critical, informed by the best available perspective on human possibilities and human limitations. One day, how soon we cannot predict, psychology and neuroscience may supply well-grounded conclusions. Until then, judgments about those possibilities and limitations can only be tentative, garnered from whatever sources have illuminated aspects of the human condition. History, anthropology, and personal experience provide fallible guides—and so too do powerful works of fiction, some of them derived from the world's religions, supplying ideas for shaping experiments and for appraising them, offering both ideals and terrifying possibilities for individuals to engage with as they try to define and pursue their own life theme.

Shakespeare and Dostoyevsky are not in the respectable business of delivering firm truths to constrain the secularist project. The pictures of humanity they offer are so disturbing that they demand engagement and reflection. The secular sense of "our own good," of what is worth wanting, is refined and deepened by struggling with their tragic vision, by trying to overcome the dangers they threaten: that confrontation restores the depth Levin's descendants take to vanish with religion. A secular worldview ought to be forged in dialogue, even in passionate interaction, with all that has been most deeply thought about what it is to be human—including whatever can be refined out of religious traditions. For secular humanism is only secondarily secular; it is primarily humane.

Sources

Lectures, even if fully written out, are not typically equipped with notes. Nevertheless, lecturers almost always draw on sources. When the time comes for translating the spoken version into a book, notes and full references can be added, even though that alters the character of the original. I've preferred to keep my text unannotated. The following paragraphs indicate the major sources on which I have drawn.

In the age of easy Internet searches, it seems foolish and unnecessary to provide particular references for cited works, especially when many editions are available and when even a technological incompetent (like me) can find one with a few unskillful clicks of the mouse. I've provided more detail when the works in question were not originally in English, less when they are classics reprinted many times. My aim has been to make it straightforward for readers to explore the background to my claims and arguments without drowning them in unhelpful clutter.

Epigraph. The passage is from *Anna Karenina*, part 8, chapter 8, translated by Richard Pevear and Larissa Volokhonsky.

Preface. The first three paragraphs are adapted from my article "Beyond Disbelief," originally published in *Fifty Voices of Disbelief,* edited by Russell Blackford and Udo Schuklenk; I am grateful to the editors and to Wiley-Blackwell for permission to use this material here.

Chapter 1. The most prominent manifestos of contemporary atheism are by Daniel Dennett (*Breaking the Spell*), Richard Dawkins (*The God Delusion*), Sam Harris (*The End of Faith*), and Christopher Hitchens (*God Is Not Great*); among these, Dennett stands out by a considerable measure for the relative sophistication of his arguments and his understanding of the position under attack. The atheist case is extended by Alex Rosenberg in *The Atheist's Guide to Reality*. On the characterization of religion and of religious doctrine, I have drawn on William James (*The Varieties of Religious Experience*), Nicholas Lash (*Theology on Dover Beach*), and George Lindbeck (*The Nature of Doctrine*). I have also learned from Mark Johnston (*Saving God*), and from Ronald Dworkin (*Religion Without God*), although our approaches diverge in important ways. The idea of basic religious knowledge is defended by Alvin Plantinga (*Warranted Christian Belief*) and by William Alston (*Perceiving God*); Plantinga's less technical discussion in *Where the Conflict Really Lies* provides a simpler statement of his claims to religious knowledge. Empirical studies of religious experience, pioneered by James in *The Varieties of Religious Experience*, are reviewed in Benjamin Beit-Hallahmi and Michael Argyle, *The Psychology of Religious Behaviour, Belief, and Experience*. A classic examination is Wayne Proudfoot, *Religious Experience*. The literature on the assembly of the Jewish and Christian canon, doctrinal shifts, and the social and political factors in the growth of these religions is enormous. I have benefited from the writings of Elaine Pagels (*The Gnostic Gospels; Beyond Belief; Reading Judas*), Bart Ehrman (*Jesus, Apocalyptic Prophet of the New Millennium; Lost Scriptures; Lost Christianities*), Richard Elliott Friedman (*Who Wrote the Bible?*), Robert Walter Funk and the Jesus Seminar (*The Acts of Jesus*), Robert Louis Wilken (*The Christians as the Romans Saw Them*), Wayne Meeks (*The First Urban Christians*), Ramsay MacMullen

(*Christianizing the Roman Empire*), Rodney Stark (*The Rise of Christianity; The Triumph of Christianity*), as well as from many other studies of issues raised in the works listed. The debate over the legitimacy of faith was begun by William Kingdom Clifford in "The Ethics of Belief," to which William James responded in "The Will to Believe"; I offer more detail about the character of this debate in *Preludes to Pragmatism*, chapter 10. Kierkegaard's classic discussion of faith is *Fear and Trembling*. Critical reaction to the broadsides of contemporary atheists is provided in Karen Armstrong, *The Case for God*, and in Leon Wieseltier's brief and trenchant essay characterizing Rosenberg's *Atheist's Guide* as "the worst book of the year" (*The New Republic*, December 14, 2011).

Chapter 2. The ideas and arguments of this chapter are developed in more detail and at much greater length in my book *The Ethical Project* (although the presentation here does refine and amend some points). Frans de Waal has attempted to describe the elements of ethics in non-human animals (*Primates and Philosophers; The Bonobo and the Atheist*). A classic discussion of changes in attitudes about slavery is David Brion Davis (*The Problem of Slavery in Western Culture*); valuable primary sources on attitudes to slavery are Mason Lowance (ed.), *Against Slavery: An Abolitionist Reader*, and John Woolman, *The Journal of John Woolman*. Scholars from a variety of disciplines have offered information about the origins of ethical life and practice: Patricia Churchland (*Braintrust*), Michael Tomasello (*Why We Cooperate*), Frans de Waal (*Good Natured*), Christopher Boehm (*Hierarchy in the Forest; Moral Origins*), Samuel Bowles and Herbert Gintis (*A Cooperative Species*), Sarah Hrdy (*Mothers and Others*). Excellent discussions of life among contemporary hunter-gatherers are given in Richard Lee (*The !Kung San*) and Christopher Boehm (*Moral Origins*). Chapter 50 of Edward Westermarck's *The*

Origin and Development of the Moral Ideas carefully describes the role of "gods as guardians of morality." The conceptions of ethics as an open-ended practice and of ethical life as improvable by the self-conscious development of method are advanced by John Dewey in *Human Nature and Conduct* and in *The Quest for Certainty*. My account of ethical truth is also influenced by William James (*Pragmatism; The Meaning of Truth*). The writings of Isaiah Berlin (for example, the essays collected in *The Crooked Timber of Humanity*) articulate the kind of ethical pluralism I have in mind. Something akin to my egalitarian ideal is endorsed by Amartya Sen in *The Idea of Justice* (a work that shares several important common themes with the approach to ethics taken here and in *The Ethical Project*). Nietzsche's critique of egalitarianism is expressed in many of his writings, but perhaps most forcefully in *The Genealogy of Morality*. My views about reasonableness and rationality are influenced by the writings of Thomas Kuhn (not only *The Structure of Scientific Revolutions*, but also the later essay "Objectivity, Value Judgment, and Theory Choice"). I discuss reasonable ways of reframing our ethical commitments at greater length in a different context in *Deaths in Venice: The Cases of Gustav von Aschenbach*.

Chapter 3. The sociological tradition in the study of religion begins with Durkheim's *Elementary Forms of the Religious Life*. It continues through the twentieth century and into the present, with Robert Bellah's *Religion in Human Evolution* being a prominent recent example. My principal sources for refined religion have been William James (*Varieties of Religious Experience*), Martin Buber (*I and Thou*), Paul Tillich (*The Courage to Be*), and Bellah's *Religion in Human Evolution;* many of the "puzzling" locutions scrutinized in the text come from Bellah (although similar language appears in many sophisticated discussions of religion). Paradigms of liberalized

Kantianism and contractualist constructivism in ethics are John Rawls ("Kantian Constructivism in Moral Theory") and T. M. Scanlon, *What We Owe to Each Other;* a related position (non-Platonist realism) is advocated by Thomas Nagel (*The View from Nowhere; Mind and Cosmos*). The pragmatist insight into the ambiguity of 'world' is offered by William James (*Principles of Psychology*), John Dewey (*Experience and Nature*), and more recently Nelson Goodman (*Ways of Worldmaking*). My thinking about world-changes has been influenced by Thomas Kuhn (*The Structure of Scientific Revolutions*). The precise delineation of a correspondence theory of truth was achieved by Alfred Tarski (most accessibly presented in "The Semantic Conception of Truth"). My general approach to truth draws from Wittgenstein's *Philosophical Investigations* (particularly the early sections) and from Michael Dummett ("Truth"). The view proposed here is developed further in my *Preludes to Pragmatism* (chapters 4, 5, and 7). The charge that secular discussions of religion often presuppose a "subtraction narrative" is advanced by Charles Taylor in *A Secular Age;* further discussion of Taylor's views is given in Craig Calhoun, Mark Juergensmeyer, and Jonathan van Antwerpen (eds.), *Rethinking Secularism.*

Chapter 4. On issues of personal death and survival I have learned from Julian Barnes, *Nothing to Be Frightened Of,* and from Mark Johnston, *Surviving Death.* A classic study of the burden of living forever is Bernard Williams, "The Makropulos Case: Reflections on the Tedium of Immortality." The importance of mattering to others is emphasized by Rebecca Goldstein (so far as I know, only in recent oral presentations). The correspondence between Thomas Henry Huxley and Charles Kingsley can be found in Leonard Huxley's edition of *The Life and Letters of Thomas Henry Huxley.* The thesis that a worthwhile life must be autonomously chosen is especially well developed in John Stuart Mill, *On Liberty*. My notion of a life theme is akin to the concept of a life plan articulated by John Rawls in *A Theory of Justice*, although I follow Dewey (*Democracy and Education*) in supposing that people's themes can evolve during the course of their lives. Religious thoughts about finitude are eloquently expressed in James's *Varieties of Religious Experience*, and especially in Tillich's *The Courage to Be*. My citation from *Doktor Faustus* comes from chapter 43 (the translation is mine). Data about the variation of religiosity with poverty are given in Pippa Norris and Ronald Inglehart, *Sacred and Secular*. For an insightful discussion of life in a thoroughly secular society, see Phil Zuckerman, *Society Without God*. The social atomism prevalent in much of the contemporary United States is forcefully discussed and analyzed by Robert Putnam in *Bowling Alone*.

Chapter 5. Charles Taylor (*A Secular Age*) contends that secular lives are "flattened." James offers the metaphor of the unheard symphony in *Varieties of Religious Experience*. The influence of John Dewey's *A Common Faith* on my thinking about religion goes far beyond the passage quoted in the text (from lecture 1). In posing questions about the effects of religious experience on human lives, I have tacitly presupposed a way of thinking about the role of biology and environment in human behavior, defended in my *Vaulting Ambition*, and a number of subsequent essays (*In Mendel's Mirror*, chapters 13, 14, and 16). Rilke's metaphor of the sustaining hands appears in his *Herbst* [Autumn]. The final chapter of my *Living with Darwin* discusses providentialism and the problem of evil. William James argues that the religiously embedded ethical life is especially "strenuous," in "The Moral Philosopher and the Moral Life." The injustice of standard Christian conceptions of the afterlife is scrutinized in David Lewis, "Divine Evil." With respect to children's appreciation of the force of ethical imperatives, I have benefited from Shaun Nichols, *Sentimental Rules*, and Paul Bloom, *Just Babies*. Jonathan Glover's *Humanity: A Moral History of the Twentieth Century* is a powerful exploration of human cruelty. Dmitri's "confession," in *The Brothers Karamazov*, is from book 3, chapter 3; again I have used the translation by Richard Pevear and Larissa Volokhonsky. Many themes of this chapter (including the role of literature in probing questions of human worth and meaning) are taken up in my *Deaths in Venice*.

Index

abolitionists, 39–40

Abraham (biblical), 4, 18, 70, 72

agnosticism, 22–23, 24, 102; soft atheism and, 23–24

altruism, 58

ancestors, 3, 62

animals, non-human, 28, 32–33, 36

Anna Karenina (Tolstoy), 123

anthropology, 159

Aristotle, 69, 77

atheism, 1, 2–3, 24, 92, 94; "soft atheism," 23–24, 25, 63, 124

Augustine, Saint, 69

Babylon, civilization of, 37

believers, religious, 10, 65; confidence of, 133–134; doctrinal profiles of, 5; evidence for existence of the transcendent and, 20–21; faith and, 18; formation of religious convictions, 7–8; knowledge from sense perception and, 11; religious experiences of, 12–13; values and, 67–68

Bellah, Robert N., 72

Bentham, Jeremy, 157

Bible, New Testament, 77, 112

Blake, William, 4

Bleak House (Dickens), 55

bonobos, 32, 47

Bradley, A. C., 79

Brahms, Johannes, 95, 102, 103, 105

Brothers Karamazov (Dostoyevsky), 149–153

Buber, Martin, 72

Buddha, 49, 58, 90

Buddhism, 9, 65–66

Camus, Albert, 158

Carroll, Lewis, 86

children, 33, 140

chimpanzees, 32, 33, 47

Christians and Christianity, 11, 14, 65–66, 103, 149, 153; afterlife doctrine, 137; denominational differences, 9; eternal continuation of life and, 95; literalism and, 4; Trinity doctrine, 23; validation of religious knowledge, 13; on value and meaning of human life, 106

churches, 106, 117, 120

Churchill, Winston S., 31

cities, settlement of first, 36, 37

civil rights movement, 117

Clifford, W. K., 17, 18, 63, 68

Common Faith, A (Dewey), 130, 141

community, 2, 94, 116, 119, 120, 154

constructivism, 85, 90

contractualism, 90

converts, potential, 14

creator, divine, 23

Crime and Punishment (Dostoyevsky), 152

culture: cultural selection, 35; evolution of, 36

Dante Alighieri, 137

Darwin, Charles R., 23, 31, 96, 105, 158

death, 4, 125, 148; comfort in face of, 2, 95–96, 102–105, 123; fear of, 96–98; of Jesus, 6; longing for immortality and, 99–100; meaning and, 101–102; premature, 100–101

Dedalus, Stephen (fictional character), 109, 131–132, 137

deities, 21, 58, 67, 139, 149; definition of religion and, 3; diversity of, 7; goodness and divine willing, 27

democracy, 48

Dennett, Daniel C., 92

destructiveness, human nature and, 141–149

Dewey, John, 47, 56, 75, 130–131, 141, 143

Dickens, Charles, 55

disbelief, active, 22

doctrines, religious, 3–6, 154; diversity of, 7, 8; doctrinal profile, 5; ethics and faith in, 61; falsehood of doctrinal statements, 63, 93; "leap of faith" and, 17, 18–19; metaphors and allegories in, 61–62, 63, 64; religious

experiences and, 13; science and, 19; specificity of, 24–25

dogmatism, 8, 12, 62

Doktor Faustus (Mann), 110–111, 113

domesticated animals, 36, 37

Dostoyevsky, Fyodor, 134, 149, 152, 155, 158, 159

doubt, 1, 3, 19; about doctrinal statements, 4; skepticism toward the transcendent, 6; strength of, 22; theological weapons against, 9

Doyle, Arthur Conan, 78–80

dreams, predictive power of, 12

Durkheim, Emile, 65

duties, 64

egalitarianism, 46, 51–52, 158

Einstein, Albert, 158

Eliot, T. S., 133

Emerson, Ralph Waldo, 66

emotions, 35, 37, 47, 51, 58, 69; attitude to the transcendent and, 66; contingent, 57

Enlightenment, 94, 106, 156

Epicurus, 134

epiphanies, 127–133

ethics: as collective venture, 140; "ethical point of view," 35; ethical progress, 30, 39–46, 53, 85–86, 142; experts and, 48; human evolution and, 33–37; irresoluble issues, 45–46; objective "external" standard for, 28–29, 31, 39, 49–50, 141; original function of, 43, 44, 48, 52; problems for, 58; providentialism and, 136; as province of religion, 27; science and, 56; social technology and, 46; strenuousness of religiously embedded ethics, 136–141; "suspension of the ethical," 65

Euthyphro, 27, 58, 67

evolution, theory of, 23, 29, 41

evolutionary psychology, 154

exclusivity (one true religion), 7

experiences, religious, 12–13, 14; conformity to orthodoxy and, 15; epiphanies and depth of, 125–133

faith, 15, 64, 71, 158; as commitment to objective order of values, 64; consolation and, 95–96; ethical legitimacy and, 16, 18, 19; "leap of faith," 17

Fanon, Frantz, 158

freedom, 106, 107, 115

friendship, 128

functional conflict, 53–54

fundamentalism, 24

Galileo Galilei, 74, 76, 81

Gandhi, Mohandas K., 158

German Requiem (Brahms), 95

God: absence of, 27; humans as children or servants of, 59

goodness (the good): divine willing and, 27; natural basis for values, 29

guilt, 35

Hamilton, William Rowan, 83–84

Handel, Georg Friderich, 16

Hansen, Hans (fictional character), 158

"happiness research," 155

Hell, 137

Herbert, George, 129–130

Hindus and Hinduism, 9, 11, 23, 65–66

history, 159

Holm, Ingeborg (fictional character), 158

Holmes, Sherlock (fictional character), 78–80

hominids, sociality of, 32–36, 41

human condition, 94, 125, 141, 158, 159

Humboldt, Wilhelm von, 106

Hume, David, 16, 134

hunter-gatherers, 34, 50

Huxley, Noel, 102, 104

Huxley, Thomas Henry, 102–104

identity, 94

infinite perspective, 136, 138

intellectuals, 1, 9, 126

interpretation, 4, 6, 19

Islam, 9, 65–66, 69, 95, 137

James, Henry, 158

James, William, 17, 45, 64, 72, 114, 134; on emotion and the transcendent, 66; on epiphanies, 129, 132; on the fervent unbeliever, 1; on origins of ethics, 138; pragmatism and, 75; problem of finitude and, 109; on religious experience as "fruits for life," 63, 87; on secular lives as tone-deaf, 124; on "strenuous" ethical life of religion, 136, 139

Jesus, 4, 5, 38, 49, 72, 90; death of, 6; as religious revolutionary, 58; role of Jews in punishment of, 14; Simeon and, 112; as son of God, 11; weeping of, 77
Jewish Community Centers, 122
Jews, 4, 14
Joyce, James, 109, 137
Judaism, 9, 65–66, 69
Julian of Norwich, 133

Kant, Immanuel, 29, 56–57, 68, 69, 85, 106
Kantian constructivism, 29, 70, 85
Karamazov, Ivan (fictional character), 27–28, 29, 149–153
Keats, John, 100, 101, 108, 111
Kierkegaard, Søren, 18, 65, 70
King Lear (Shakespeare), 143–149
Kingsley, Charles, 102, 103–104
knowledge, 9, 11, 12, 20; faith and, 15, 16; progress and, 41; search for, 2; surprises in history of, 19; validation of religious knowledge, 13
Kröger, Tonio (fictional character), 158
Kuhn, Thomas, 56

labor, alienated, 115, 120
labor, division of, 36, 37, 158
language, 81, 156; acquisition of, 34; truth and, 77, 79, 86, 87
Lessing, Gotthold Ephraim, 156
Leverkühn, Adrian (fictional character), 110, 113

literalism, 4, 25, 71, 72, 118
literature, 143
love, 71

Machiavelli, Niccolò, 145
Makropulos, Elina (fictional character), 113
Mann, Thomas, 110, 113, 116
Marx, Karl, 120, 158
materialism, 121–122
mathematics, 82–84, 85, 86, 88
Mather, Cotton, 40
matter, indivisible parts of, 23
meaning, of human lives, 101–102, 138, 151; epiphanies and, 127–133; finitude (impermanence) and, 110–115; question of the good life, 105–110
medicine, progress in, 41
memory, 10
Mendel, Gregor, 30, 40
Mesopotamia, law codes of, 36, 39
Messiah (Handel), 16
metaphor, 109, 124, 136, 155; Hell as, 137; and literal interpretations of religion, 4, 59; refined religion and, 62, 68, 89, 93, 133, 134; and religious doctrines, 62, 63, 64, 66; resurrection of Jesus as, 6
Mill, John Stuart, 106, 107, 115, 157
monotheism, 5
morality, building blocks of, 32
Moses, 77
mosques, 120

Muhammad (the Prophet), 4, 5, 72, 77, 90

"multiple realities," 73, 76, 78, 81, 92

music, 95

Muslims, 4, 11, 103

mysteries, 4, 73

"mythical truth," 92

Nathan der Weise (Lessing), 156

naturalism, ethical, 53

nature (natural world), 19, 72

neuroscience, 159

New Testament, 77, 112

Nietzsche, Friedrich, 52, 158

normative guidance, 33, 34

original sin, 143

Orwell, George, 158

Paleolithic era, 33, 36, 39, 119

Pascal, Blaise, 22

Paul, Saint, 71

perception, 10

philosophy and philosophers, 29–30, 42; "ethical point of view," 35; philosophers as elite, 48; question of the good life, 105–107; refined religion and, 69; "true myths" and, 76

phlogiston "principle," 80, 81

physics, 10

physiology, 10

Plato, 27, 69

Platonism, 82

poverty, urban, 117

pragmatism, 45, 75

primates, 32, 33

progress, 39–45, 63, 85–86, 138; purifying progress, 92, 121; "subtraction narrative" and, 91

property, private, 36

Prospero (Shakespearean character), 112, 113

Proust, Marcel, 158

providentialism, 134, 135

psychology, 5, 10, 28, 159

punishment, eternal, 137

Qur'an, 103

reason (rationality), 29, 35, 54, 57; Kantian philosophy and, 85; Kantian practical rationality, 56; transcendent as realm of, 69

reform, social, 55

religion: abolition of slavery and, 40; "advanced" and "primitive," 9; atheist views of, 2–3; community and identity associated with, 94; "core doctrine" of, 62; as corrective to materialism, 121–122; death of, 93; definition and characteristics of, 3–6; ethical truth and, 84; fundamentalism, 24; life transitions and, 95; original egalitarianism undermined by, 38; pervasiveness across human cultures, 142; psychological needs of potential converts, 14, 15; science at war with, 5; social structures provided by, 2 religion, refined, 64, 85, 88–91; comfort in face of death and, 105; community and, 119; cosmopolitanism and, 88, 94; "different worlds" and, 73–74; ethical authority and, 93; history of, 72; hope and confidence supplied by, 133–134; identification of values and, 67–71; secular commitments differentiated from, 64–67; soft atheism and, 63; as system of practices and commitments, 61; "true myths" and, 156; world construction and, 74–81

responsiveness, 48, 147; mutual, 143–144; problem of limited responsiveness, 50, 58, 71, 157

rewards, eternal, 136–137

Rilke, Rainer Maria, 133

Roman Empire, 14, 106

Röntgen, Wilhelm, 30, 40

sacred places, 7, 8, 62

Schopenhauer, Arthur, 143, 144

Schweigestill, Max (fictional character), 110–111, 113, 115

science, 1, 73, 91; discoveries in, 30, 40; fantasies of complete final theory, 75; natural world and, 9, 19; religion at war with, 5; "scientific revolutions," 56; surprises in development of, 19, 23; testing of conclusions, 10; world construction and, 80–81

scriptures, 6, 8, 62; ethics and, 93; evolution of scriptural canon, 13–14;

literal versus metaphorical/allegorical readings of, 4

secular humanism (secularism), 25, 57, 67, 92, 116, 159; death and, 96, 97, 125; doubt and, 1, 3; ethics and, 29; meaning and, 122; objections to, 46; providentialism and, 136; refined religion and, 72; soft atheism and, 23–24

self, the, 74

self-restraint, 33

sex, 51

Shakespeare, William, 113, 158, 159

shame, 35

Shelley, Percy Bysshe, 129

Simeon, in New Testament, 112, 113

skepticism, 3, 6, 20, 58

slavery, 30, 39, 40

social justice, 117

Societies for Ethical Culture, 122

Socrates, 27, 31, 49, 58, 67, 109

soft atheism, 23–24, 25, 63, 124. See also agnosticism; atheism

suffering, human, 139, 140

suicide, 96

superstitions, 7

symmetry, of beliefs, 8, 9, 63, 93; appeal to privileged knowledge and, 11–12; as unsolved problem, 12

synagogues, 120

Taylor, Charles, 124, 126, 127, 128, 132

technology, 41, 43, 71

Tennyson, Alfred, Lord, 99

theology, rational, 9, 20, 21

Tillich, Paul, 72, 109

Tithonus (mythological), 99, 100, 113

tolerance, 7

Tolstoy, Leo, 1, 92, 123

trading networks, 36

transcendent, the, 3, 4, 8, 10, 149; autonomy and, 109; diversity of conceptions of, 62; elements of religious life and, 65; ethical values anchored in, 28–29, 30; ethics and, 90, 136; lack of evidence for reality of, 20, 21–22; as mystery, 103; as realm of reason, 69; religious knowledge and, 9; reports of encounters with, 14; revised notion of, 23; skepticism toward, 6; as source of values and virtues, 64; two-tier universe and, 66, 69, 70; validation processes for claims to encounter, 13

"true myths," 73, 76–77, 88, 155, 156

truth, 6, 62, 63, 102; ethical, 38–42, 45; factual, 77, 78, 81, 84, 92, 120; fictional, 79–80, 86; "higher truth," 72; language and, 77, 79, 86, 87; march of progress and, 45; mathematical, 82, 85, 88; "mythical truth," 81; pragmatic constraint on, 77; religious experiences and, 15; transcendent, 8–10; as ultimate value, 92

Unitarians, 122

Ur, civilization of, 37

value judgments, 28, 53, 54, 123; humanity at center of value, 59, 69; progress in ethical project and, 85; religious grounding of, 57–58; secular Kantians and, 57

Whittier, John Greenleaf, 105

Wittgentstein, Ludwig, 81–82, 83

Wollstonecraft, Mary, 49

women, status of, 39

Woolman, John, 40, 49

Wordsworth, William, 129

"world, the," 74–76

writing, invention of, 36